STRAIGHT FLOSSIN'

AND OTHER STORIES
OF THE AMERICAN WEST

DANNY NIELSEN

WHISTLING
RABBIT
PRESS

Straight Flossin' and Other Stories of the American West
Copyright © 2022 **Daniel Patrick Nielsen**

Contact the publisher at info@whistlingrabbitpress.com
Contact the author at https://dannynielsen0.wordpress.com

Paperback ISBN: 978-1-950835-03-4
eBook ISBN: 978-1-950835-04-1

Publisher's Cataloging-in-Publication data

Names: Nielsen, Danny, author.
Title: Straight flossin' and other stories of the American West / Danny Nielsen.
Description: San Diego, CA: Whistling Rabbit Press, 2022.
Identifiers: ISBN: 978-1-950835-03-4 (paperback) | 978-1-950835-04-1 (ebook)
Library of Congress Control Number: 2022938501
Subjects: LCSH Nielsen, Danny. | West (U.S.)--Description and travel. |
West (U.S.)--Environmental conditions. | Habitat (Ecology)--West (U.S.)
| Deserts--West (U.S.) | Essays. | BISAC TRAVEL / United States /
West / General | NATURE / Regional | NATURE / Essays | NATURE /
Ecosystems & Habitats / Deserts | NATURE / Ecology
Classification: LCC F591 .N55 2022 | DDC 978--dc23

Illustrations by **Sunny Noel Sawyer**
Cover design by **Victoria Davies at VC Book Cover Designs**
Interior design by **Arc Manor Book Design**
Author photograph by **Peter Nielsen**

Printed in the United States of America

Published by
Whistling Rabbit Press
San Diego, California
whistlingrabbitpress.com

——— **For Skylar** ———

Contents

A Beckoning on the Horizon

I HAVE spent the last decade studying the plants and animals that carve out a living in the deserts of the American West. I have seen wildflowers blossom from the drying crust of spring and stared as bighorn sheep scaled cliffs. I have listened to bird song in the predawn darkness. In the desert, ribbons of green cut through planes of red and brown. A day of sun and heat can turn quickly to a black, cold night blanketed by an ocean of stars. I have fallen in love with mountain skylines and marmalade sunsets. But I have also found frightening beauty in the metropolises emerging from this land of stark contrast. On moonless nights in the vast wilds of the West, the luminous domes of cities pierce the sky. Inside each bubble is a microcosm of the human experiment.

A light bubble radiates above the horizon of a desert night. It glows beyond mountain peaks and ridge lines. To the casual observer, it may look like a moonrise, showcasing the brilliance of Earth's natural satellite. To the wanderer of the open road, the beacon is a landmark. For the weary traveler, a milepost: *"Only 90 minutes left to home."* For the lonely, it is a connection to the nameless forms of humanity, searching for meaning in the pall of urban life. To the misanthropic dirtbag, the light in the distance is a reminder of the chaos they escaped to chase bucolic fantasies in the hinterland. A vantage point from afar. Outside looking in, one considers their place.

Outside the light bubble, along desolate stretches of road shared with wildlife, you expand your consciousness. You ponder the stars. The beauties of creation are revealed to those lucky enough to behold the vastness of the universe. To the perceptive, realization dawns of one's inconsequence in the Cosmos.

As you approach a light bubble, it slowly grows. A singular radiance becomes a formless wash of light. You pass a nebulous threshold. Thousands of stars and the band of the Milky Way are cashed in for artificial light and the industrial vibrations of civilization. A narrow road becomes a network of traffic signals and cars. Fast food. Fast cash. And the all-too-often mindless scuttling of humans from one place to another. The excesses of consumption are displayed on every street corner. Flashing lights and neon signs advertise cheaply made, low-priced stuff. Souvenirs that promise fleeting pleasures rather than lasting happiness. Workers scramble to and from shifts. Homeless toil in the streets, their livelihood in the hands of passing strangers. Inside the light bubble, peace, quiet, and beauty are gone—bedlam reigns. Meaning and purpose, monetized by the greedy, are sold like commodities. The worth of a life is measured by its contribution to the ever-growing economy.

I have ventured through many of these light bubbles in my years traveling the Western US. Perhaps the most singular, and stark, is the one that envelopes Las Vegas. Like a galactic center, tugging on its surroundings, it lights the horizon from any direction. From the north, it shines above the sagebrush sea of the Great Basin Desert. From the northeast, it gleams above the red rock of the Colorado Plateau.

Observed from the south, the apparition glows above saguaro cacti in the moonlit Sonoran Desert. And on approach from the west, the luminosity burns above the ancient creosote shrubs and Joshua trees of the Mojave Desert. From all directions, the backdrop of Las Vegas hovers on the horizon, a premonition of its ubiquitous influence on the landscape. Vast tracts of desert are consumed to provide solar and wind energy. Mountains are excavated for minerals and resources or hollowed into giant tombs for nuclear waste. What little water moves along the surface is usurped with surgical precision—allocated to urban centers by men who assumed power from those rendered powerless. But this limited resource is not enough. Vast underground aquifers are tapped, with giant straws, to quench the unquenchable.

Those have been my thoughts as I drove dark and lonely highways by myself, far from the nearest city. Listening to whatever plays on the crackling radio, I have found the conspiracy-laden talk shows of the AM dial provide an apropos soundtrack to the mystery that lies ahead. But other nights I have rolled along with the windows down, listening only to the air whip through the car. Occasionally stopping along a deserted stretch of road to stand alone and gaze into the sky. The sound of silence in my mind at times interrupted by the howl of a coyote or the screech of an owl. At peace, searching the heavens above, I have found meaning in my own insignificance.

The following are stories of some of my travels through the Western US. Many are set within the Mojave Desert of California and Nevada—where I have spent much of the last decade. Others are more broadly set within the West. They do not recount events and people precisely but are inspired by real people and real places. They follow a common thread: the people, the places, and, often, the contradictions of the American West.

Keith's Place

THE FIRST time I drove to Kelso Valley, I hadn't a clue where I was going. Other than virtual explorations on Google Earth, I was only familiar with the area from reading the research of my new grad school advisor. It was someplace in Kern County, California; four hours south of Bishop, where I was then living. Between Bakersfield and Ridgecrest, this site was tucked in a corner of the desert at the southeastern margin of the Sierra Nevada, smack dab in the middle of Nowhere. Those were the objective truths I knew of the area from looking at maps and browsing the web. But maps don't say who lives in Nowhere. Nor can they tell you why.

I had become obsessed with the surrounding Mojave Desert—in fact, with all the deserts of the American West. Five years earlier, while working on my master's degree, I lived in the sprawling metropolis of Phoenix, Arizona, in the heart of the Sonoran Desert. I spent the school months in the suburb of Mesa, and during summers I worked in portions of the desert where the isolated corners of Arizona and Utah meet southern Nevada. A place where the valleys of the Great Basin, the red rock of the Colorado Plateau, and the rugged Mojave Desert unite in the remote landscape that had aroused my Southern sensibilities years earlier.

Growing up, and before I spend time in any desert, I lived in Alabama. The wooded plains of the South provided endless adventure for youthful escapades, but views above the forest canopy were seldom seen. When I was in high school my parents moved the family to Utah, via road trip in our van. Shortly after entering the beehive state from Colorado, I saw a man, miles from the nearest town, jogging along the side of the highway. His sunburned and sinewy body was quickly dwarfed by the expansive panorama beyond. The snowcapped La Sal Mountains resembled phantoms on the distant horizon as they floated high above the surrounding sea of red. Strange plants grew from the sandy soil and stretched their branches toward the blue sky as if in a struggle to endure.

It was there that I began my love affair with the lands of—only to the uninitiated—vast dry nothingness. I was to learn the difference between the subtropical climate of Alabama and the arid West, where drought is the baseline. When it *does* rain, the desert floor comes alive with carpets of green and yellow, red, and purple. When precious liquid falls from the sky, the magic of the desert overwhelms the senses. The smell of sagebrush and creosote. The blossoms of saguaro cactus in spring. But precipitation aside, the immensity of these landscapes took my breath away. The brilliance of the night sky was unmatched. Somehow, even the improbable cities carved in the inhospitable landscape provided inspiration.

After I finished my master's degree, I spent the next five years deciding what to do next. Did I really want to pursue a PhD? I continued to feed my desert addiction with itinerant jobs throughout the West. The appeal of more school grew during those years in the wilds. One temporary job after another began to feel unsustainable. Gradually, perhaps out of madness, the idea of spending years digging deep into questions that few other humans would even consider asking seemed like the logical next step.

Almost by chance, I found an opportunity to study desert woodrats as a dissertation project. As a seasonal field technician for the California Department of Fish and Wildlife in Bishop, I had been assigned to accompany a retired mammalogist to trap voles in the middle of Owens Lake. On a blustery October evening, I drove down Highway 395 and met him near Lone Pine. We caravanned into the dry lakebed and parked along the wide shoulder of a causeway as giant gravel trucks barreled by. I felt as though we were in a Mad Max set. As we set traps and made plans for checking them in the morning, I learned that a former student of his was looking to recruit a PhD student for a funded project. The field work would be someplace only a couple hours south of Owens Lake, in the Mojave Desert. I sent an email, and that was that. I started field work only a few months later.

The study site was at a hybrid zone between two species of woodrats. In a remote location where the desert meets the mountains. What better place to satisfy my habit than the middle of Nowhere? After some research and planning, my advisor told me to get familiar with the location. With the enthusiasm of a religious disciple guided by some higher meaning, I loaded my truck and disappeared into the landscape.

By then, I had spent enough time in the remote desert to know something of the kinds of people an arid landscape attracts. A certain mentality is required. Or maybe, a certain mentality is sculpted from the harsh environment. The heat, sun, and wind do strange and wonderful things to the human brain. Why is there a pony-drawn carriage traveling the

7

remote highways of Nevada? I do not know, but the coachman seems nice enough. Why the Lemon House of Cartago? The peculiar yellow inn made from the recycled remains of a radar from a military base is one incarnation in the cycle of human innovation. And why did artist Michael Heizer dig two enormous holes in the blank desert for no apparent purpose? Seventy-five miles from the Las Vegas Strip, his Double Negative earthwork consists of two trenches 1,500 feet long, carved into opposing sides of Mormon Mesa. Empty space in a landscape that, to the unobserving eye, also appears empty, but is in fact full of life.

Those are manifestations of the beautiful madness that materializes after years in the heat and sun. But in the madness lies a dark underbelly. Communities destroyed from within after being neglected from outside. Mobile meth labs occasionally explode, and drug-addled tweakers destroy the homes in which they live. Young men scrape together a living on occasional work, unemployment benefits, and petty theft. A property owner fires over your head when you unwittingly trespass on *their* land. But sometimes, these are the same people who offer to pull your truck from the sand. Or, when you nervously catch their eye, they greet you with a wave and a smile. In my travels, I have learned that the desert can be home to the best and the worst of what humanity offers.

I was thinking of beauty and madness as I navigated the sinuous canyon road to Kelso Valley for the first time. Alone, I had remained as discreet as possible while driving through the sparsely inhabited canyon. Joshua trees, yuccas, creosote, and other hardy plants populated the sides of the narrow road. Among a small community of sunbaked homes, a dilapidated trailer sat in the middle of a fenced property. At the front of the yard flew a pair of flags—Gadsden and Confederate —a clear message to passersby to *Stay the Hell out*.

But downcanyon, in Weldon, I had friends. Having ventured in previous years to the South Fork of the Kern River, I had met the biologists and managers of the Southern Sierra Research station and adjacent Audubon Kern River Preserve. A pocket of riparian habitat about 3,000 acres in size surrounded by agricultural fields, the Preserve envelopes a stretch of the river and provides a temporary home to thousands of migrating birds. Among them is the endangered southwestern willow flycatcher, an inconspicuous songbird that travels thousands of miles a year between the southwest—where they nest—and South America. But the Preserve is also a seasonal home to eclectic biologists from all over the world. Their own peregrinations take them around the globe, as if playing tag, in search of those birds.

The director of the research station was always thrilled to talk science and chat about birds. She was athletic—often coming or going from softball games—and a great wildlife biologist. Over the coming years, she would offer the station house to my crew to use the internet, take showers, and enjoy the simple pleasures of evaporative cooling.

I also met Reed, the good-humored manager of the Preserve. He kept a closely shaved beard and often wore a ball cap over his neatly trimmed graying hair. Frequently wearing a Hawaiian shirt, to my mind, he should have been captaining a yacht somewhere in the Caribbean. Sipping a Mai Tai before setting sail into the sunset. As the field station bunks were usually full, Reed let us camp on the Preserve property in an area he'd mowed beneath the cottonwood and willow trees. It was still hot, but the shade was preferred to the exposure of our study site.

My research took me to the area during colder seasons as well. One December, I drove down for a stint of field work between the end of fall classes and the holidays. Reed needed help with the Christmas Bird Count, an annual tradition,

9

that to birders seems akin to taking the sacrament. But these zealots are always happy to take along a novice to count the birds. Reed mentioned an area next to my field site, so I volunteered. He instructed me on how to find the spot, tucked in a small side canyon along Kelso Valley Road. He called it, as did everyone else at the Preserve, "Keith's Place."

"Keith's been up there since the mid-'90s," said Reed. "He's a World War II vet. Ninety-two years old. I like to check on him every now and then. Make sure he's still alive," he said, before I started up to the property. Keith's Place was tucked inside a canyon accessed by a narrow two-track road I had scarcely noticed previously.

Keith was small in stature but huge in his passion for birds. He lived alone on several dozen acres of land near the base of Mayan Peak. Among other chores, he maintained a small spring that fed the riparian habitat. All the work he did on his property was "for the birds." We toured the oasis, following the stream bed that flowed from the spring and looking for birds along the way. I barely kept pace as we navigated the vegetated channel. He pointed to where a pair of owls nested in a cottonwood tree. The channel was dry above the spring. I followed him through a break in the steep banks to the ridge above, and we circled back around to his house.

The one-bedroom ranch house sat under large cottonwood and willow trees. A solar panel was fixed on the south end of the roof. There, sunlight poured through a clearing made by the two-track driveway that led to several small structures in varying stages of decay. His cat came out to greet us. I thought it funny for a bird enthusiast to keep a pet cat. Most cats don't share humans' scruples about killing birds, but they do make good company for a desert loner.

Warming rays of the late morning sun found their way through the canopy and thawed the cold morning air, so we sat on the porch, in close view of his bird feeders. We chatted about woodrats and the birds while we tallied our counts. I offered Keith a beer, but he declined, stating he only drank red wine, so I took the nonagenarian's choice as subtle health advice and opted instead for a glass of water. I had coffee to finish anyway. Having driven past his small paradise countless times over the previous two years, I wished I had met him sooner.

I would make many more visits to Keith's Place over the next year. Living alone, my new friend was always eager for a visitor. He kept a notepad on his coffee table which served as a guest log—to keep his family from worrying about his isolation in the desert hills. He made me sign in each time I visited. I frequented his place in the hot summer afternoons, dragging along anyone who dared suffer the desert heat with me. We talked about life, his world travels during the war, and his quest for exotic birds after the war. His singular attention to the birds was so great that only after multiple visits did I learn he had two children. A daughter in Southern California and a son in Colorado. Keith told me about the Honor Flight trip he took with his daughter to DC. "A few years ago," he said. Funny, as it turned out it had been a decade since his trip, but I guess years have a way of blurring when you have lived a long and colorful life.

Once I found him sitting on his couch with the fan turned on his bare chest. A glass of room temperature red wine at his side. "Go away, Sun," he hollered out his window. Even inside, it was over 90 degrees. He was simply waiting for the long summer day to pass into the cool desert night. I grabbed a beer and joined him in the exercise in patience.

I once asked him what he thought about the windmills on the southern margins of Kelso Valley. My own feelings toward them were still somewhat ambivalent. I had never seen the landscape without them, and renewable energy seemed the way of the future, if humans were going to curb the effects of climate change. Keith hated them.

"It just means more people," he said. "It's always about more people." It struck me as odd. Not that I hadn't heard the arguments against renewable energy before. Solar and wind farms are harmful to local wildlife and wreck the wilderness, but their effects on mitigating climate change are important. Given his environmental tendencies, I had imagined he would take a more nuanced perspective. But Keith went straight to the core of the problem, with not much room for argument.

He was right. The ultimate cause of many environmental problems seems to circle back to rapid human population growth, regardless of the forms of energy used. In areas with limited resources, such as Southern California, the apparatus of progress reaches far into the wilds. Charismatic politicians promise eternal economic growth. But that growth requires more energy, in any form. So policymakers and planners had found part of the solution in Kelso Valley, where turbines convert perennial winds into energy to feed perpetual growth. The residents of this remote outpost are now connected to a city hundreds of miles away. Keith didn't care for it. He could do with fewer people on Earth. More for the birds.

Keith's Place became a mandatory stopping point on my travels in and out of the valley. A refuge. Where I had once avoided other people, I was drawn to Keith. His years on Earth gave him a perspective that I wanted to learn from. For almost as long as I had been alive, he had shared this sanctuary with the wildlife he loved. Keith made me reconsider the answers I thought I had about the meaning of life and the path forward for humanity. He revealed the complex nature of humans' relationships with each other and with the land they inhabit. I learned to look for and find beauty in these contradictions of the human enterprise. Somewhere there is a notepad collecting dust with my name written in its pages. The sole record of the lessons I learned from a friend. After he passed away, the two-track road to his property was chained off. Keith's Place was now exclusively—"For the Birds."

Fire in the Desert

THE SUN dropped below the ridge as I placed the last trap. I walked to my favorite rock where a warm slab of granite provided an unobscured view of the desert below. In the east, the cloudless sky faded through pastel shades of blue and purple in the last rays of sunlight. The crescent moon was already high in the sky, and Mars was beginning to shimmer. Occasional wind gusts ripped through the pines above me while I gazed at infinity.

My shoulders were sore from hauling woodrat traps up the steep hillside while navigating boulders and logs and sliding on the fine granitic sand that covered everything. I was ready for a beer and some rest before checking traps in the early morning hours. I looked to the north and tried to ignore the plume of smoke that had been growing all afternoon. A fire had started earlier that day near Lake Isabella, over 20 miles away to the northwest. Was it growing rapidly? Or did it only look that way as smoke fanned out in the prevailing wind currents high in the atmosphere? My optimism told me it was the latter, but my gut told me it was the former, and I was beginning to worry about the situation.

I started back down the hill with my empty trap bag, thinking how much easier it would have been to haul the empty bag up the hill. But the physical exercise was a welcome break from sitting in front of a computer screen. I spotted the headlights of a vehicle dropping into Kelso Valley on the dirt road from the north. There were two ways in and out of the valley—the north pass by the Pacific Crest Trail which would be impassible if the fire continued to grow, and the southeast where the road vanished into the windmill-covered hills. My friend Cassidy was planning to meet me and Michael, who was working with me as a field technician that summer. I assumed the car was Cassidy's and headed back to camp. I was excited have a beer with him and get his take on the fire situation.

He waved through an open window as he parked in the dry wash where Michael and I had made camp. "Cassidy, how the hell are ya?" I asked. "Want a beer?"

"Sure thing, buddy," he replied as he stepped out of his SUV. His red hair stuck out in multiple directions from beneath a ball cap.

"Michael and I just finished setting the lines. Between the two of us, nearly a hundred," I said proudly. Our routine had been to set traps in the evening just before sunset, eat dinner and rest for a few hours, then check them starting around midnight.

"Is that a lot?" Cassidy asked.

"It'll make for a full night of work," I said regretfully as I realized how long it would take. I quickly changed the subject. "Hey, what's your take on this fire?"

Cassidy was stretching, bent at the hips, touching the ground. Michael was organizing his truck cab, getting ready for bed. He opted to skip dinner and go straight to sleep in the twilight of sunset. I'd never figured out how he was able to sleep in the slightly reclined position afforded by the driver's seat of his small truck. Tonight, I suspected it would be pure exhaustion.

Cassidy grumbled as he stood upright. He cracked open his beer and looked toward the column of smoke. "Shit man, it looked like it was rippin' pretty good, but it's way out by Lake Isabella," he said.

I took another sip of my beer and watched the smoke rise into the atmosphere, flatten out, then flow southward like an airborne river of soot and particulate matter. "We were down in Weldon at the research station when it started this afternoon. They said something about a kid with fireworks," I said uneasily.

"I had the radio on," said Cassidy, as he searched the back of his SUV for a sweater. "Said it was growing fast but didn't know how it started. It's windy as hell out there today."

"Yeah, been windy here too, only got a break from it just before you got here. Still some gusts, but it's calmed down a bit," I said with an eye on the smoke. "You don't think it'll spread all the way up here?"

"Hard to say. It'd need to cover a lot of ground, but…" his voice trailed off as his face grew serious.

"Dammit," I groaned at the thought of the remote possibility. "When we got here earlier, the wind was blowing the smoke this way. Blocked the sun, turned everything orange. Apocalyptic," I said with a forced smile. "But the winds died back, and it cleared some. Seemed like we'd be okay."

"Yeah, I think it'll be all right," said Cassidy. "There's a bunch of mountains in between. I don't think it'll get here." His words calmed me some, but he continued, "I told Mara I'd call her and let her know we're okay."

I realized if Cassidy's girlfriend wanted an update, I should probably let my fiancée know too. "We'll have to drive back to Weldon for that," I said. "No signal up here."

"All right," he said. "That'll be good. We can get a better idea about the fire. But I think we're fine," he reiterated.

I was starting to regret all those traps. How stupid I was to go ahead with setting them. But I had been eager to get to work. Any new grad student would be. I checked on Michael. He was just tucking into his front seat nest, and I caught him before he donned his night mask.

"Hey, Michael," I called through his window. He looked up, startled. "We're gonna drive downcanyon and see about this fire and make some calls," I said. "We should be back in about two hours." He nodded, pulled down his night mask, and rolled over. *"Goddam, how does he do it,"* I thought.

I hopped in the SUV with Cassidy. He executed a three-point turn, slotting the rear of the vehicle between two rabbitbrush shrubs, and gunned it out of the wash. It was now almost nine o'clock, and the drive would take the better part of forty-five minutes. The sky was dark, and stars were making their nightly rounds. The smoke was beginning to fade in the darkness, but large gaps in the starry night sky indicated its presence. The Big Dipper was missing its handle. I glanced over at Cassidy and was startled to see him in large wire-rimmed glasses.

"Damn, Cassidy. I forgot how you look like Jeffrey Dahmer in those things," I said, attempting to bring some levity to the situation.

"Hey, shut your foul mouth," he grinned. "I need these to drive at night."

It took us five minutes to crest the pass of Kelso Valley, giving us our first glimpse of the canyons to the north. Now on paved road, Cassidy hugged the shoulder as he raced around tight turns. The radio struggled to find a signal and settled on a curious medley of stadium country and fanatical voices of radio evangelists. Maybe the maniacal voices were right. Maybe it was the "End of Times."

We had gone only 10 miles or so when we followed a bend in the road and approached a small community of homes. I looked ahead to a glowing ridgeline and felt my stomach sink.

"Shit," I said. "Cassidy, the fire is climbing that ridge."

"Jesus Christ," he said as he slowed to a stop on the roadside. Tendrils of flame were visible through an orange haze. The fire looked to be within 10 miles. We spotted a Bureau of Land Management fire truck in the driveway of a nearby ranch house. Cassidy slowly pulled in behind it and set the parking brake, leaving the engine running. Trees danced in flashing lights.

I stepped from our vehicle and approached the truck. "Hello," I called to the firefighter behind the steering wheel.

"Hi," she said as she stepped down from the vehicle. Her eyes pierced me from under a yellow helmet, then she turned sharply and made for the house.

"We've been up in Kelso Valley," I said as I jogged to keep up with her, although I knew any questions about this fire had just been answered. "About 10 miles upcanyon."

"We are advising everyone to evacuate," she said promptly. "This fire is growing fast, and the wind forecast isn't good. The situation is extremely unpredictable."

Cassidy and I read each other's minds. He had already shifted into reverse and was looking through the back window. I shouted our thanks to the firewoman as I ran back to the car. Other cars passed along the road on their way out of the community.

"Let's go!" I said as I jumped in the passenger seat and slammed the door shut. "We gotta get Michael," I said to Cassidy as he stepped on the gas. "And close those damn traps too." If the fire *did* burn through the valley, it could very well kill wildlife, but I sure as hell wasn't gonna let any helpless creatures cook in my traps.

"Yeah, yeah, yeah," he said as he flipped the SUV around. "We should have time. There's at least 15 or 20 miles between the field site and the fire. It won't move that fast," he said. "The fire can't move that fast."

Cassidy careened through sharp turns in the road as we sat silently with our thoughts. Calls home would have to wait. The sky was thoroughly black now, with only the soft unnatural glow of the crescent moon. As we pulled back into camp, I bolted to Michael's truck. He was sound asleep, unaware of our arrival, and completely oblivious to the deteriorating situation. *"How the hell does he do it?"* I wondered frantically, feeling a moment of regret before I pounded on the window.

"Michael," I hollered as he jolted upright and grabbed for the mask covering his eyes. "We gotta get out of here!" He looked perplexed and squinted his eyes before shielding his face. I realized my headlamp was blinding him, so I turned my head. "Hey, we need to leave. This fire is spreading fast, and it's too close now. But we have to close the traps first," I said.

"Okay," he said as he rubbed his eyes with one hand and opened the truck door with the other.

"Cassidy, you help Michael close his trapline down here." I wildly gesticulated toward the wash where Michael had set traps earlier that day. "There're about 60 traps. We don't have time to pack them up. Just close 'em and leave 'em," I said.

Scrambling in the darkness, our efforts to mobilize seemed as hopeless as herding cats. Cassidy scrounged for a water bottle, slid a headlamp over his forehead, then looked toward Michael for direction. Michael was standing against his truck, still groggy and blinking his eyes. I ran to my truck and took a gulp of water and tossed the bottle into the back with all my gear. I was glad both Michael and I had been sleeping in our trucks; all our things were already loaded, and we could roll out quickly. We all kept looking toward the north and the fire. A faint glow of orange continued to radiate above the distant ridgeline, but we couldn't make out any flames at this distance. *"Extremely unpredictable,"* I thought.

"All right, let's do this!" I said as I ran toward the hill. Headlamps flickered across the desert as the others stumbled toward the wash. "Move fast, guys!"

We moved westward, our progress slow in the dark. Michael and Cassidy walked up the slight incline of the desert wash as I trotted to the base of the hill. A nearby mockingbird must have sensed the looming threat as it looped through its musical repertoire like a broken record. I found the beginning of my trapline and began following its circuitous path up the boulder-strewn hillside. The traps had been set for less than three hours, but in the first half of the line I had already captured a half dozen woodrats—a good haul for this line of work! "Be free and godspeed, little friends," I said as I opened trap after trap. I grimaced as I thought about all the lost data. "But it's too late for those thoughts," I said aloud and continued up the hill.

Although I was unrestrained by the weight of traps, I struggled to find my way through the maze of boulders, all while keeping watch for rattlesnakes—in or out of the traps. *"God, I hope I don't have to wrangle a rattler from a trap tonight,"* I thought. From atop a large granite boulder, I looked below to the headlamps of Michael and Cassidy bobbing haphazardly along the desert floor. To the north, the orange glow seemed to be drawing closer, aided by the prevailing winds. I scanned across the valley and saw the flashing lights of the fire truck moving along the road, followed by a line of headlights. I started to worry I was losing count of traps but continued to trudge uphill, stumbling between them. I sighed with relief as I found the last set. Trembling with adrenaline, my hands fumbled as I closed the latches in the glow of my headlamp. I left the pair of traps on a shelf of rock and ran downhill, back toward the eerie scene below.

At this point, I didn't care if something got left behind. I broke camp in a rush, throwing any remaining bits of gear into the back of my truck. A quietness had descended upon the wash. Even the mockingbird had calmed in the nearby tree. But as I looked up and to the north, the orange glow hung ominously over the strange calmness.

"That's the last one." Michael's voice cut the silence. He and Cassidy appeared out of the dark a few moments later, breathing heavily.

"Let's get the hell out of here," I said as I closed the back of my truck. "We're gonna go south. Follow me." We would have to follow Jawbone Canyon Road out to the southeast, through the wind farms. It was now past midnight, and the drive to Mojave would take at least an hour and a half, assuming the road wasn't blocked by evacuees already ahead of us. A flat tire or dropped axle was all it would take to hold the whole convoy up for hours.

We caravanned through the two-track to the main dirt road and turned south. I dodged jackrabbits and kangaroo rats as I sped along. Far in front of us, the fire truck and its small caravan of evacuees crested the southern pass and disappeared into the hills beyond. With our safety in sight, I exhaled and loosened my grip on the wheel.

At the pass, I stopped along the side of the road. We stepped out of the trucks and stood in the darkness, looking north. I had heard that large wildfires can create their own weather and imagined a hellscape of heat, smoke, and fire devils that firefighters battled as they attempted to protect the nearby communities. My anxiety about the field site burning to the ground was quickly replaced by concern for the people whose homes were either destroyed or, very likely, would be. We watched in silence as the sinister orange glow illuminated billows of smoke rising over the mountains in the distance.

"Jesus," said Cassidy. "That fucking thing may just burn into the valley."

"It just may," I said as I got back in my truck. I pressed my back into the seat and exhaled. "It just may. And we still got a long way out of here." I turned on the ignition and cued up the Grateful Dead. "Fire on the Mountain" seemed fitting for the occasion.

Back on the road, we descended the canyon to the east, toward Mojave. The red lights of windmills blinked throughout the surrounding hills as I continued to swerve around wildlife. A poorwill flitted from its roadside roost, eyes glowing red in the headlights. Eventually, our small convoy reached the bottom of the canyon where we turned south on Highway 14.

Out of the protective terrain of the canyons above, the prevailing winds ripped crosswise along the highway. I dodged herds of tumbleweeds crossing the road. We were now straight flossin' through the last 20 miles of desert into Mojave.

The town of Mojave resides on the western edge of the Mojave Desert and sits between two highways and a bone-rattling railroad line. I had only travelled through it a couple times before and knew little of its past or present. But, from my brief experience, it was just the kind of dodgy desert town that lured me in with its eccentric flaws. Such small desert outposts, I had found, were far more tantalizing than the manicured sterility of suburbia.

The buzzing sign of a Motel 6 greeted us at the north end of town, and we pulled into the parking lot one after another. Young men with facial tattoos loitered near the far corner of rooms while cockroaches skittered along the exterior walls. The wind whipped up a mess in the parking lot. Sprinklers watered the air, and mist hit us from every direction. Waves rippled in the swimming pool, and I considered jumping in. Water that had been pilfered from the desert now danced in a depraved celebration of man's dominance over the harsh landscape. The same wind that was driving an inferno through the desert now pinned multi-colored plastic bags to the fence line in an opulent display of consumerism.

Cassidy ran toward the lobby, and Michael and I stayed back to unload the trucks. In our hasty retreat through the desert, my gear had taken a pummeling. Bins had tipped over and spilled their contents. I opened the back hatch to the camper shell of my truck, and the wind immediately sucked a plastic lid into the parking lot. It skated along the moistened black top before disappearing down a storm drain.

"Holy shit!" I shouted as I quickly grabbed my bag and closed the hatch.

Michael, suffering similar challenges, retreated to the homey interior of his truck cab, and wrestled with the door. "I'm just gonna wait in here," he said as he managed to slam the door shut.

Cassidy rejoined us in the parking lot. "Got a room on the first floor," he yelled through the wind and pointed around the corner of the building.

By the time we piled into the room, it was well past two a.m. Michael jumped in one of the beds and passed out. Never to be heard from again that night. *"He must relish the musty motel bed over his truck,"* I thought. Cassidy and I unpacked a few things before confronting the tempest once more to find beer at the nearest all-night convenience store. We were exhausted, but I was still riding an adrenaline high, and sleep would have to wait until after a round of drinks. We drank our beers in silence before dozing off. We slept soundly. Not even the thunder of trains would wake us.

The next morning, we walked across the highway for breakfast at a diner run by a few cheery ladies. We wolfed down breakfast burritos and coffee before Cassidy left for home. I wanted to hang around for the afternoon, see if I could wait out the fire. I had hopes that we might be able to get back into the valley. And since I had only hired Michael days earlier, I felt obligated to come up with something for him to do.

I obsessively checked the internet for updates on the fire. I even called the local offices of the BLM. After a few hours, I accepted the fact that we wouldn't be returning to the valley for field work any time soon. We went our separate ways. Michael drove back to his home in Southern California. As I cruised north to Reno, I kept my eye on the never-ending plume of smoke to the west. I would be fortunate if all I lost was my field site. Maybe I could just write my dissertation on post-fire effects in a small mammal community. "*Hell, maybe every dissertation that relies on field work will become a fire effects study,*" I thought, considering the ever-growing area of scorched land across the western US.

That fire took from the landscape, the wildlife, and the people that occupied that remote corner of the desert. It became known as the Erskine fire and had started when a broken power line hit a tree near Lake Isabella. The strong winds caused the fire to grow to over 8,000 acres within the first few hours. It would eventually burn over 45,000 acres during the following two weeks, destroying 309 buildings and killing two people. Before it stopped, the fire came within six miles of my field site. This small corner of the desert I was falling in love with was safe for now. But, like so much of the parched West, what was spared now might go up in smoke next time.

Unknown Unknowns

ONCE, EARLY in my PhD adventures, I drove across the Mojave Desert to meet an old friend from Utah. Tara, a high school and college classmate, was now a few years into her graduate program. Her field work took her to the remote desert which was just the kind of place I was falling in love with. My exploits had only just begun. I had been reading literature and had visited my field site a few times. I had already even collected a little hard-earned data. I was formulating research questions and thinking like a scientist. Or so I thought. But I was only a few months in and hadn't taken any coursework yet. Now, I wanted to get a sense of the work of a bona fide doctoral student.

Naturally, when Tara invited me to visit her study site, I jumped at the chance. I didn't need much prodding to ramble through the desert. With restless energy, fanned by the naïve idealism only a new grad student can possess, I raced across Owens Valley, climbed over the Inyo Mountains, and drove through a network of highways across Nevada. I was eager to see her work, get some ideas for my own, and maybe learn something along the way. Her site was at Brigham Young University's Lytle Ranch Preserve—a field research station in Utah, near the Arizona and Nevada border, and where back roads pass seamlessly among all three states. The closest towns of significance, each about an hour away, are Mesquite, Nevada and Saint George, Utah. The bordering region of Arizona, known as the Arizona Strip, is a vast swath of wild Mojave Desert broken by rugged and remote mountains. The middle of Nowhere. Other than a couple small communities, not much else exists there but creosote, cactus, and polygamists. All struggling to survive in a beautiful, yet hostile landscape.

As I drove mile after mile, late April showers turned to deafening thunderstorms. Storm clouds gathered across the panorama before me, sucked in moisture, and reached their crescendo atop lofty peaks far in the distance. Torrents of rain fell from the skies dozens of miles away. Flashes of lightning. Rays of light from the late afternoon sun pierced through clouds. Swatches of golden radiance illuminated the mountains to the east. Who needs the movies when you have this? The best show on Earth. I skirted the north end of Las Vegas and turned eastward toward Utah.

I passed through Mesquite, Nevada, where the local economy thrives on vice. Only a 40 minute drive from Saint George, Utah, renegade Jack Mormons partake of cheap alcohol, loose slots, and the occasional clandestine foray into the nightlife. But outside the town of golf resorts and casinos peddling $5.99 steak dinners, the surrounding desert is mostly empty. North of Mesquite, I entered Arizona. Shortly after, I turned north on Old Highway 91, drove through the small community of Beaver Dam, and cruised through open desert.

After crossing an invisible border into Utah from Arizona, I turned off the highway and drove 10 more miles on a dirt road. It was wide enough in most places for two lanes but was heavily washboarded from spring rains and traffic. During ideal conditions, the road didn't require any special vehicle; a sedan could easily make the trip. But during or after a deluge, a benign dirt road in the desert can become a nightmare. Chunks of earth tear away from the shoulder. River crossings form where there once was little more than a trickle. Motorists are sometimes swept away in torrents of mud and rock and vegetation. Thankfully this road was spared these ravages, and, although it was bumpy, I covered the mileage without mishap and reached a clearing on a plateau above the ranch. It was late, and only a few lights shone through the bunkhouse windows below.

To avoid waking the slumbering biologists, I parked in a glade surrounded by juniper trees for the night. The rain had stopped, and stars appeared in the gaps of clouds drifting overhead. The brilliant points of light shimmered in the cool air. I sat on my tailgate, sipped a cold beer, and watched the Celestial display until my eyes grew heavy. I crawled into the back of my camper shell and left the hatch open so I could watch the night sky as I fell asleep.

I awoke to birdsong and the tangerine glow of dawn. The rising sun evaporated the previous night's rain, and a thin fog rose into the air. I tumbled out of my truck and boiled water for coffee. Heriberto, the ranch caretaker, whistled below. His melodies ascended the forest canopy and blended with the hissing of my stove. Once my coffee was ready, I drove down the hill to the ranch.

The property was a menagerie of buildings and irrigated fields. Chickens scratched for food in a coop behind the ranch house. Numerous cabins were tucked under the cottonwood and willow trees, and a recently finished bunkhouse stood in a large clearing. In front, a gravel parking lot accommodated field vehicles. All around lay the tools of real field biologists. Weather stations. Automated rain gauges. Pickup trucks with labels: "For Official Use Only." The land gently sloped away, and fruit tree orchards, melon patches, and fields of alfalfa stretched out from the stream that gave life to the land.

Heriberto had moved to Utah from Mexico and now lived with his wife at the ranch year round. He was tall and maintained his muscular frame with physical demands of ranch work. He wore a neatly trimmed mustache that accentuated his friendly smile. Graying hair was just visible under the edge of his cowboy hat. I approached as he stood near the ranch house talking to a few people with binoculars around their necks. One man held a spotting scope.

"Good morning," I said, interrupting his conversation with the birders. "Have you seen Tara?"

Heriberto shook his head. "They head into the field early. Before sunrise."

"Darn. Well, thanks," I said.

"They usually come back for lunch," he said. "Around 10:30 or 11."

"Okay, thanks. I'll just wander around until they get back," I said.

I had my binoculars, and so I spent the morning hours birding and looking for lizards and snakes and other wildlife that flourished at the verdant ranch. Around eleven I wandered back toward the houses. A summer tanager had caught my attention, and I stood staring through my binoculars into the large cottonwood tree that kept the bunkhouses in shade for much of the day. Just then I heard a truck and a loud *rat-a-tat* as it crossed a cattle guard. I looked down from the tree and saw Tara in a tie-dyed T-shirt and ball cap in a pickup truck. Inside the cab with her sat three younger girls.

"Danny! I hoped we'd see you here." Tara smiled from the window. "I haven't had a chance to check my phone all week."

"Well, I figured I'd find you out here. I left a message a few days ago but knew you likely didn't have cell service." I leaned against the side of the truck. "Hi y'all," I said as I looked into the truck cab.

"Everyone. This is Danny, my old friend from high school. The one I was telling you about the other day," she said to the others. "Danny, this is Bailey, Becca, and Ashley. They're undergraduate field techs for the summer." She looked back at me. "Did you just get here?"

"I got in late last night and slept up on the plateau," I explained. "I guess I was so tired I didn't hear y'all on the way out. How'd it go this morning?"

"It was great. Sorry you missed us. We finished some transects up on the rim that we started yesterday. We bailed when the thunderstorm came in," she said.

"Yeah, it was a big one," I said. "I was worried about the road."

"Eat lunch with us," she said. "After, you can go with the girls to collect the Sherman traps, if you want." They had been trapping small mammals and, in a hurry to escape the previous day's storm, had left a pile of them a few miles away.

"Sure, sounds fun," I said.

We ate lunch under the cottonwood trees as a breeze kept us cool. Tara said she and her husband had kids now and she hoped to finish school in another couple years. She had been a high school science teacher before going to graduate school and thought she might go back to teaching, but she wasn't sure. She liked research. She asked what had possessed me start a PhD.

I don't think I really knew why. Maybe I still don't. But I was drawn to it. Maybe the way a moth is drawn to a candle. I had a lot of ideas swirling but nothing formulated. And what I lacked in certainty, I made up for in excitement about the unknown future that was unfolding ahead. I rambled on about how years of idle wandering and indecision made me eventually realize what I thought I wanted. How I thought it made my choice more logical. I wanted to understand the desert and the organisms within. I wanted to ask questions that no one had thought to ask before. I wanted to find meaning in a complex world. My response was the typical romanticized interpretation of science. The kind that one can only hope to keep a small portion of after the absurdities of the world begin carving away at the blissful ignorance of youth.

We finished lunch, and the field techs got straight to work preparing to go back into the field. I could see they were hard working and disciplined. They meant business. With the kind of focus and determination that I could have used in earlier years, they began loading gear. I helped lift a box into the side-by-side, then climbed into the back with Ashley. Becca sat up front as Bailey pulled herself into the driver's seat. She turned the ignition and offered us a menacing grin before taking off like a race car driver and leaving a trail of dust. I held onto the roll cage as we careened around the gate and up the switchback toward the top of the canyon rim.

"So, you're enjoying working out here with Tara?" I yelled to Ashley.

She looked at me but hadn't heard. I loosened my white-knuckle grip and leaned a little closer to repeat my question.

"Yeah, I love it out here," she hollered with a smile.

We had now climbed out of the canyon and were perched on the upland mesa with 360-degree views of the desert. Distant mountains rose gently from the desert floor into the sky where afternoon thunderstorms formed. We walked along the desert floor, enjoying the plant life, fertile from spring rains. It had been years since I had spent much time in that corner of the Mojave Desert, and I had forgotten how many plants there were to know. Of course, the students knew the plants, and I stopped every 10 feet and asked what I was looking at. Purple and yellow flowers of *Krameria* and *Coleogyne* blossomed from lush green foliage. We spotted the red berries of *Lycium*. And scattered everywhere were Joshua trees, the sentinels of the Mojave Desert. Like a Seussical creation, their distorted forms rose from the desert floor, their outstretched arms heavy with white fruits.

In my brief time with these three undergrads, I could see they were sharp and that I would learn more from them than they from me. I walked with Ashley who had a look of deep contemplation and spoke with depth and clarity.

"What do you like most about science?" she asked.

"Shit, my charade is up," I thought. *"Maybe I have no clue?"* It was a broad question, and I paused before I answered, seriously beginning to question what I knew.

"I suppose…" I said with a pause. "What I like most is the never-ending nature of it. We may never run out of questions to ask. So long as we keep an open mind."

She smiled and didn't disagree, but remained silent, as if thinking it over. We reached the end of the line, and each of us, arms full of traps, turned and walked back. The others asked me about graduate school and how to prepare and what classes are best to take. I happily pretended to have useful answers.

"Well," I said. "I started out taking classes that seemed interesting. Plant taxonomy, mammalogy, herpetology. Then when I finished my undergrad, I wasn't sure what to do, but graduate school seemed like one of the few options I had. And I was rejected plenty of times before getting in," I clarified.

The clouds started to break, and it seemed as though whatever storm had been brewing was dissipating. They rolled off over the mountains to the west, making the peaks look larger and even more isolated. Back at the bunkhouse, we reconvened with Tara before making a short trip to her experimental plots just above the ranch on the canyon rim. From atop, the sandstone bluffs rising below were now glowing red in the afternoon sun. A green ribbon of riparian vegetation meandered through the wash.

"So, what's your 30-second elevator pitch?" I gave Tara a shit-eating grin, knowing this was an annoying question.

"Everyone always asks that." She smiled while unloading gear before taking a breath and saying in a rush, "I study competition of invasive species after abnormal fire events in a desert ecosystem."

"Wow," I said. "You've done that a few times."

I looked across the maze of experimental plots and was overwhelmed by the size and scale. The two large plots were each large enough to build a house on and were bordered by fences of chicken wire and sheet metal flashing. Each plot was then further subdivided into four smaller squares.

"So, what exactly is going on in these?" I asked.

"Each of these experimental areas is split into four different treatment groups. This array allows us to measure the relative influences of small mammals and fire on competition among various species of invasive plants," Tara said as she pulled on a spool of wire.

I considered the huge installation. Two segments had been burned, and two remained unburned. Likewise, small mammals had been removed from two while two were left alone. This provided a simultaneous look at the combined influences of presence or absence of both fire and small mammals. Tara was particularly interested in post-fire invasion and competition among non-native grasses, such as red brome, cheatgrass and Mediterranean grass. I was getting first-hand experience with the required fine-scale vegetation monitoring, precipitation experiments, and other time-consuming aspects of ecological field research. What would appear on paper as a relatively simple study design stretched out before me into a full-time operation for a small army, let alone a single student and a handful of underpaid field technicians. I did my best to help Tara and the others mend holes in the fences to keep the mammals out of the control plots.

"What has been the most challenging part of graduate school so far?" I asked Tara. I assumed she'd had some hard courses. Real ass-kickers. The kind that force you into a her-mitage, deep within the musty library, to study advanced sta-tistical analysis or neo-contemporary conservation biology in a globalized world.

Tara looked out at the others, cutting wire and mending fences. Behind them, the work site fanned out the length of a football field, requiring attention to every square inch. The sun cast a golden glow upon the operation. I thought about how they had been up since before dawn. She stood up with a pair of wire cutters. "The biggest challenge has just been having enough help to get all of this work done. And done well," she said. "We work dawn to dusk every day, and still run out of time to finish all the work." Resolutely, she turned back to join the others at the fences.

I was surprised. I thought hard coursework and writing papers were the cornerstone of grad school. Sure, field work was hard. But it was supposed to be fun, right? Everyone knows that science is difficult, requiring meticulous record keeping and deep thought. But I hadn't considered the sheer physical labor of it.

Beyond the bluffs of the ranch to the west, the sun began to approach the horizon, stretching our shadows along the desert floor. The mountains to the east glowed red, bidding us good evening as we finished patching the fences and stashing the equipment. I now questioned my motives. I knew a PhD would be challenging. But the apparent impossibility of it all? Maybe I couldn't pull it off? A twinge of anxiety tempered the anticipation of my own adventure as I realized what Tara was facing.

The next morning, after saying our goodbyes, I traveled westward, covering miles of open road across the Mojave Desert. Somewhere along the way I caught an episode of a podcast, that, perhaps by cosmic intervention, I needed to hear. The host talked with one of a pair of psychologists who had studied a form of cognitive bias. They conducted experiments on students and found that those who thought they excelled in a particular subject area often performed worse than those who doubted their own abilities. Essentially—trust those with crippling self-doubt? Apparently, the guy said, this form of ego afflicts everyone, eventually. Most of us know what we don't understand and, if we have the motivation, can learn it. But what about unknown unknowns? He proceeded to suggest that everyone will eventually get caught in this trap. Ultimately, our confidence in the things we know will blind us to the things we don't know. Even for the humble among us, there may be things we simply cannot recognize. *"Is this real?"* I thought. *"Can't be."*

Real or not, this cautionary tale bit into my naïve idealism. Just a couple days before I was blasting through the desert riding a joyful wave of obliviousness. I was on my way to visit an old friend, take some notes, and maybe learn a thing or two. Now I was thinking about all the things I didn't know. The mysterious challenges of graduate school that I would face. The unexpected hurdles. The surprises. Perhaps these were valuable life lessons too. Rather than hide behind answers, never stop asking questions. If I were to succeed in this, I'd need more than a strong work ethic and determination; I'd need humility. I could never forget that the more I learned, the more I would realize I didn't understand.

Strange Stewards of the Desert

NEIL AND I had been driving for hours, and it was now 9:30 p.m. The orange glow from the dash illuminated the interior of the car, and sad songs played on the radio. An oldies station from Barstow on the AM dial. A timeworn cowboy wished he'd lived a fuller life. Outside, stars dotted the night before fading into the light bubble of Los Angeles to the west. The Big Dipper, Cassiopeia, Mars and Jupiter, and many other celestial guideposts twinkled brightly. I started mumbling.

"Light bubble?" Neil broke his silence behind the wheel. "What are you talking about, light bubble?" He chewed a piece of dried mango. Blond hair hung loosely across his face. He had a muscular yet lean frame with broad shoulders.

"Well, ya know, LA, Vegas…All these big ass cities in the desert. When you are driving along at night, you can see their light bubbles for miles," I said.

"Oh, I see." Neil grinned slightly as he tried to see it in his mind. "Like a snow globe." He tossed some roasted almonds in his mouth.

"Yeah!" I turned in my seat and smiled. "That is a perfect way to describe it."

"Light bubbles..." I continued rambling. "You only see them when you are out here, right? As you get closer, they get larger until, eventually, you're part of them. Then the stars disappear. Maybe you still see a few bright ones. Part of the Big Dipper. But mostly the night sky fades away into the artificial glow of the city and you lose it all. And then you're just part of it." I talked on as he attempted to stay interested. "I think I like outside the bubble better."

Neil turned off I-15 and headed south on a cracked and narrow road that intersected the dry channel of the Mojave River and continued into the desert. Sand blew across the road as we crossed the desiccated riverbed. Unkempt salt cedars formed islands. Mesquite bosques lined the channel. I rolled the window down as we slowed for a left turn onto a dirt road. The warm desert air rushed in, carrying with it the pungent odor of creosote. The haunting call of a poorwill rose from somewhere in the darkness.

"Whoa, this is a shitty road." Neil gassed the engine as we fishtailed over a sandy patch.

"Wouldn't that be something, huh, get stuck out here in the dark. In a shithole of sand," I said. "Hitch a ride and probably get picked up by a meth cook or something." I chuckled at the insanity of it while dust, illuminated by the headlights, blew over the windshield. I quickly rolled the window up.

"I think we're getting close. Hopefully," I said as we continued along the narrow lane until it reached a small house.

Outside the house, the wind rapped a splintered sign against a wooden post. The words were faded by the desert sun and barely legible—"Camp Cady." We had arrived at the State-managed desert riparian wildlife area. At that time, Neil and I were temporary field technicians for the California Department of Fish and Wildlife. We were underpaid and overworked, but the job took us to beautiful, yet often overlooked, desert landscapes. Places that often laid bare the contradictions of modern life.

In the morning, we would survey for the endangered southwestern willow flycatcher. These small drab birds were migrating, and our job was to see if they were using the riparian habitat at Camp Cady. I had emailed the caretaker, Bruce, but with no reply I wasn't sure he knew to expect us.

"Who is this Bruce, anyway?" Neil shifted the car into park and turned off the ignition.

"I think he is a volunteer caretaker for the Department of Fish and Wildlife," I replied. "It wasn't very clear on the website. Apparently, he stays out here by himself most of the time."

"You think he got the message we were coming?" Neil asked as he opened the door.

"Maybe. I think his wife calls him every few days," I said. "To give him his email messages and make sure he hasn't died." I stepped from the car.

It was past 10 p.m. Through the howling wind, bellowing calls of bullfrogs came from ponds hidden somewhere in the night. The moon shone below a mountain ridge to the east. Buildings, visible in the soft glow of a single lamp post, stood in varying degrees of dilapidation. A low mechanical rumbling drew my attention to a clearing where the shadowy profile of a tower stood against the night sky. I hadn't the slightest idea what it was—the eerie darkness of this strange place would hide its secrets until morning.

We weren't sure where we were welcome to sleep. Usually, I was happy to sleep under the stars, but I wasn't eager to be sandblasted all night in the relentless wind. We recalled hearing something about a bunkhouse.

"The lights are on over at the house," Neil said. "I'll go see if Bruce is around." He started for the small white dwelling. I followed behind.

A lamp post illuminated the faded green shutters of the house. Insects danced in the light. The long branches of a desert willow twirled about a low fence. We stepped inside the gate and onto a well-watered patch of lawn. A sign directed patrons to the correct side of the lawn to relieve one's pet. An assortment of cacti and other succulents lined the inside of the fence. A bird flushed from under the porch awning.

Neil stepped up to the door and knocked. Through the window, flashing lights danced off the walls and the sound of a buzzer followed the muffled voice of an excited gameshow host. Several silent moments passed before a woman's voice was followed by a ding and applause. Neil knocked again. This time I heard floors creaking and the shuffle of feet. The door opened, and a man looked out through the screen door.

"Bruce?" Neil asked.

"Yes, good evening." He smiled. "Neil and Danny?" he asked as he ushered us in. Bruce was a large man. His grey hair was cleanly trimmed above big eyes that dominated his weathered face. What looked like possible melanoma spotted the end of his rounded nose, and his ears drooped a little. A white T-shirt pulled tightly around his stomach was tucked into denim jeans. He shuffled away from the door in his stocking feet as we stepped inside.

A bottle of table wine stood half full on the coffee table. An empty jar sat on a coaster, leggy red streaks down its sides. The smell of cooked meat mingled with the musty essence of the old house.

"So, you're gonna survey for willow flycatchers tomorrow?" he asked. "That's just great. I love those little birds." He ambled back to his seat on the couch.

"That's the plan," Neil said. "We're gonna survey the habitat that runs along the north end of the ranch. We plan to start around 5 a.m." He yawned.

"If you find any, it'd be great for getting more funding for habitat restoration projects," Bruce said. He became animated at the thought of finding these rare birds. "We have lots of good birds out here. White-winged doves, ash-throated flycatchers, verdin, phainopepla, tri-colored blackbirds." He poured another glass of wine as he listed off names. "I am hoping to begin more projects this summer, if we can get the money."

"Do you want to join us in the morning?" I asked as Neil hinted at the door with tired eyes.

"You go on without me," he said. "I've got some things to do around here. But I'll be around all morning. Come find me when you're done." We turned toward the door. "Oh yeah, almost forgot. Stay in the bunkhouse," he offered before we stepped outside.

"That would be great," we replied together.

"Well, it's just behind the house, toward the river. You'll need the key. Let me go and find it." Bruce disappeared into the back of the house. The noise of drawers opening and closing lasted for about a minute before he returned.

"Ah crud, I dunno where the key is. One of the groundskeepers probably misplaced it. Let me keep looking." He wandered into the back room again. The sounds of shuffling papers and metallic clinking ensued before he gave up. "You may just want to go see if the door is already unlocked," he said.

We walked through the darkness to the bunkhouse. The front door was locked, and Neil started around the house to find another entry. The small building was in poor condition—a state of deterioration that results from years of sun, heat, and wind in the Southern California desert. A torn screen covered a window. I tugged on the latch and startled a night lizard who zipped into a crack in the concrete. The window opened and I inched it up until the opening was large enough to climb through. Halfway in and working my hips over the sill, I heard footsteps from the back of the house.

"Neil?" I was hanging through the window.

"Hey, I found an open door in the back," Neil said. His headlamp illuminated the front room I was attempting to enter.

"Sweet," I said. I squirmed the rest of the way through the window. I dusted off my shirt and pants as I stood upright and looked at Neil. "Jesus," I said. A cloud of dust glowed in his headlamp. The place looked like a cesspool of hantavirus and any number of other animal-borne diseases.

The interior was hot and musty. Smells of decaying life seemed to be trapped in the walls. Faded papers near the entryway did indeed warn of hantavirus. Toward the back, I found a sooty television in a room filled with leather furniture, tables, desks, and piles of old National Geographic magazines. Everything with a healthy coating of grime. I flicked on the TV just to see what would happen. An eerie red glow radiated from the screen, reflecting off dust floating in the stagnant air of the room.

I explored and looked inside one of the bedrooms. Paisley quilts sagged over twin beds. I sat on one. A plume of moth wings lifted into the stale air and floated gently to the floor. I gladly stepped back outside onto the front porch.

"I think I'll sleep out here after all," I said to Neil as I took a breath of fresh air. "Pretty bad in there."

Neil was already rolling out his bed. "Yeah, the wind has calmed some. It shouldn't be too bad," he said as he crawled into bed.

"There's a dead mouse in the kitchen garbage," I said. "I think I'll just boil water for coffee out here tomorrow."

I found my camp chair, grabbed a beer from the cooler, and sat down. As I sipped from the frosty can, I realized the porch ceiling blocked my view of the sky, so I moved into the open gravel parking area. I leaned back and gazed at the sea of stars above. A small satellite slowly tracked across the heavens. The Milky Way burned a broad path before it disappeared into the light bubble of LA. I sipped the last of the beer, then made my bed and lay down. I slowly fell asleep as wind rustled leaves of nearby cottonwoods and bullfrogs continued their nocturnal refrain.

The first sound I heard when I woke was the dawn song of a western kingbird. Like a small clown laughing after huffing a balloon full of helium, it cackled in a nearby tree as I sat up and rubbed my eyes. I fumbled for my glasses and looked around—all the night's secrets now lay exposed. Rows of corn covered a large field beyond the gravel parking area. The crop would provide bait, and cover for hunters, for dove hunting season. Beyond, sunflowers stood in rows, faces pointed toward the morning sun. I could still hear that low rumble, and now in the morning light, I identified its source. A pump house stood like a sentinel over the property. A rickety wooden ladder ascended its side to a flat top. Grinding away, its motor pulled water up from the ground for irrigation. I walked to the edge of the damp cornfield and paused. At my feet, a single datura plant displayed its radiant white flowers in the morning sun.

Sometime later, Neil and I were on the hunt.

Fitz-bew…Breet…Breeeeet…Fitz-bew…Fitz-bew…
Fitz…Fitz-bew…Fitz-bew…Fitz-bew…

"You hear him?!" I asked as Neil fidgeted with his binoculars. A southwestern willow flycatcher sang from somewhere in a tree canopy near the middle of a small marsh.

"Hold on." He readied his binoculars. "OK, where was it singing from?" His eyes disappeared into his binoculars.

"It sounded like it came from that Goodding's willow." I pointed to a tall tree rising above the rushes. The rising sun warmed my back as I squinted into my binoculars toward the tree.

"Do you see him?" Neil stepped through some low branches for a better look. "These limbs are in the way." He swatted branches with his free hand.

"I see him!" I said. "He's about five meters up the willow tree."

He flapped out from the tree in small arcs, hunting insects, before returning to his perch. We stood shoulder to shoulder for several moments watching this repeating pattern before the small bird vanished into the thick shrubs below.

Neil's pencil danced along a data sheet as he checked boxes. "Four willow flycatchers! Hell yeah," he said. The sun was now above the tops of the cottonwoods to the east. The temperature had climbed to the upper 90s, and a gentle breeze cooled my sweaty skin.

"I'll go find Bruce," I said.

"Okay, I'm gonna go read," Neil replied as he bit into an apple.

I drank water from my bottle and walked toward the house. The birds had gone silent, except for the melancholy murmur of mourning doves. A jet plane softly rumbled overhead, leaving behind a white streak. Behind Bruce's house, near a tattered barn, I noticed a white four-door truck parked by an RV.

Bruce's front door was open, with just the screen door closed to keep the flies out. The television was on, and a late-morning infomercial touted the benefits of an all-natural ginkgo biloba weight loss supplement.

"You watchin' this shit, Bruce?" I teased from the screen door.

"Ah hell, Matlock reruns were on earlier, then this crap," he called from the kitchen. "Come on in, Danny. I was out early this morning on the other side of the property working on the irrigation for the corn field."

"Who's staying in the big trailer out back?" I asked.

"Oh yeah." Bruce gave a sigh and grimaced. "That's Clint. He's a USDA biologist. He comes out here every month or so."

Bruce joined me by the front door, and we both heard the rumble of a diesel engine. The ash-throated flycatcher nesting in the porch darted from under the awning.

"Uh, this is him," he said. "I'll tell you more in a bit."

Bruce watched as Clint stepped through the gate and came over to greet us. He was tall and pencil thin. His short dark hair was topped with a USDA ball cap, and he wore a long-sleeved shirt tucked tightly into his jeans. Squinting through glasses, his brown eyes crinkled at the corners. He held himself with in a dignified posture and gave us an awkward smile.

"Good afternoon, Clint. This is Danny. He's surveying for southwestern willow flycatchers," Bruce proudly introduced me.

"Hi, Clint. Jealous of your trailer out back...I noticed it earlier," I said and grinned at him.

"Yeah, that's me back there," he replied with a toothy grin and adjusted his pants.

"You work for the USDA? Whadda ya do?"

"I work on raven control," he said. Bruce flashed a disapproving look as Clint continued with excitement, "Surveyors come out and locate raven nests, particularly the ones that eat tortoises...Ya see, some nesting pairs, not all, but some, eat desert tortoises. And you know, they're endangered. So, the surveyors look for desert tortoise shells around their nests and record the location." Clint looked sheepishly at me.

I quickly glanced at Bruce. He shifted his weight and chewed on his lip. I might have caught an eye-roll.

Clint went on, "So then, I get all the locations for ravens that eat tortoises and—"

"He shoots them," Bruce interrupted.

"Well, yeah," Clint interjected. "If a pair of birds eat tortoises, I shoot them. Only the birds that eat tortoises though." He made sure to clarify that point.

"Well, getting hot out," Bruce said as he turned toward the door. "Thanks for stopping by, Clint. Have a nice afternoon."

Clint grinned self-consciously and called after him, "Okay, you have a good day too, Bruce. And nice meeting you, Danny."

"Nice meeting you, too, Clint. Enjoy your afternoon," I said as he climbed into his idling truck.

"Well," I said to Bruce. "I better go find Neil and pack up." The temperature was now triple digits, and the only sounds of life were insects buzzing. I walked across the property, following shade where I could. The low groan from the pump house pulsed rhythmically.

It was funny to me, that little interaction. Bruce was fond of all the wildlife on the ranch. Even tortoise-eating ravens. After all, ravens are native inhabitants, carving out a living in an unforgiving land. They are often found in Native American art and have been a part of the western landscape since long before European settlers spread like wildfire into every corner of the continent. Raven populations expanded in their steps, increasing alongside the ever-growing human population of the American West. Clint's job was perhaps a necessary evil. A reactionary solution to the chronic growing pains of human enterprise in the arid West. Maybe he understood this. But, like a kid yearning for approval from his father, he wanted to be appreciated.

I wasn't against the killing of ravens. I could see the need. But it was a pathetic attempt to mitigate the larger problem of human disturbance across the landscape. Like patching a hole in the side of a dam with bubblegum. Society's insatiable appetite for growth has carved up the desert. The amazingly adapted organisms that call the desert home are doing their best to maintain existence. More development, more energy, more outlet malls. Our solutions to the resulting environmental problems often fall short. Our answers to the problems we create generate new problems. New questions.

Neil and I were just temporary visitors to this oasis. Like the birds we surveyed in this forgotten nook of the Mojave Desert. But those endangered birds rely on riparian habitat throughout the desert West for migration and nesting. A pitstop for the travel-weary puffballs. Each spring they fly north from the tropics to breed, before heading back south for winter. Carved into the desert landscape of the American southwest, the improbably hospitable Camp Cady is just one of many important patches of habitat for these birds and other winged creatures. And Bruce was there for all of them.

Finding Shade and Losing My Mind

I ROLLED around in my tent, struggling to get comfortable. The sun was up, and I'd miscalculated what its angle would be at dawn. By 8 a.m., my tent was a sauna. We had set up camp the previous night in a dry wash that provided shelter to a small oak tree. The wash, the lowest point in the surrounding desert, was a cold sink. The small oak tree, surviving off ground water deep below, provided shade. But the rays of sun that made it past the small tree cooked my tent like a tray of mashed potatoes under a heat lamp at a casino buffet. Everyone else's tents were still enjoying shade deeper under the tree, and from the sound—or lack thereof—they were still asleep. Eventually I found my phone, relegated to being an expensive watch in the remote desert, and looked at the time: 9 a.m. *"Damn,"* I thought. *"Haven't even slept four hours yet."* As was typical for my crew, we'd worked all night trapping woodrats, almost until dawn. Now, we struggled for what little sleep we could get. Our tents were crammed around the base of the small tree at different angles, in a strained attempt to make use of what little shade it would provide in the morning hours.

I looked at my truck parked nearby, and, by some stroke of luck, it was still in the shade. I crawled out of the tent with my bedroll and climbed into the back of the truck. A shrike roosted in the oak tree and let out an occasional screeching call. I closed the shell to keep the flies out and tried to fall back to sleep. The wind gently rocked the truck as I closed my eyes and began to drift into a light slumber. In no time, a gust of wind woke me. As I sat up and looked around, I realized I had peeled off most of my clothes and was lying on top of my bedroll in a growing moisture ring of sweat. I took a gulp of water and re-checked my expensive watch. It was just before 10 a.m. I gave up on getting any more sleep and climbed out of the truck. I stood at the tailgate and stretched for a moment. The others were still sleeping in the shade. Looking around, I noticed the beer cooler was taking on direct sunlight. Concerned for the well-being of its precious contents, I looked at the sun angle and the tree, and moved the cooler into what I judged to be the thickest shade that would also last a good while.

Keeping track of shade while working and living in the desert is as much an art form as it is a necessity. Finding the deepest shade for stashing a cooler full of beers, or keeping a tent cool, requires considerable consideration. You see, shade is a commodity in the desert, and there are as many options as there are three-dimensional objects on the landscape. You, the consumer, have some shopping to do. First, you must judge the deepness of the shade. How much shelter from the oppressive sun will this shade provide? Once you have found a satisfactory patch of shade, you then must consider the length of time you need its services. As sure as the earth moves around the sun, a sweet patch of shade won't look the same in an hour. You must ask your little patch: "How long will you last?" Or, if you are using the shade for sleeping, "What will you look like at 9 a.m.?" These are critical questions that only a desert rat will consider.

Sometimes, though, you should admit defeat and move on. I decided that any efforts for more sleep were fruitless and pulled my chair around to the shady side of the truck. A six-foot-long, three-foot-deep, and rapidly disappearing rectangle on the west side of my truck was just big enough to hide in for a few more minutes. I leaned back against the side and watched a few clouds slowly drift above the mountains to the west. Cactus wrens were busy with their morning chatter, and the shrike still let out its occasional shriek.

After several minutes, I decided to make coffee. As much as hot liquid might sound unbearable in the desert heat, my caffeine dependency superseded logical forms of thinking. I put a small pot of water on the stove and poured coffee grounds into my French press. As I waited for the water to boil, I looked to the craggy peak on the northeastern rim of the valley. Rising from the valley floor, shallow washes meandered haphazardly across its face. Toward the top, blocks of granite guarded its peak from all directions. It looked to be about a half-dozen miles or so from our camp. In my sleep-deprived state, I made the executive decision, then and there, that I would set off on a venture to the top of this obscure desert peak.

Having downed my coffee, I heard sounds coming from Jason's tent and crept quietly over to the door flap. "Hey, Jason," I whispered. "I'm going for a run. I'll be back in a few hours."

"Huh?" He was still waking up.

"I'm going out for a few hours. I'll bring the two-way radio."

"Okay. Sounds good," he replied in a muffled tone.

I loaded my daypack with water, snacks, and the radio. It was now well past 10 a.m., and the sun was shining in full glory high in the eastern sky. One could argue that setting off on a run at such a time and in such a place was not the best decision. But the only people capable of that argument were sleeping. So, I set off.

Cactus wrens continued their chattering as I jogged along the two-track that wound through the rabbitbrush and Joshua trees. Winter rains had been good to the annual forbs, and mats of flowers covered the desert floor between shrubs. Sunflowers carpeted the mountainsides above the valley.

The first mile was flat before I reached Kelso Valley Road. The wide dirt road was well groomed and served as the western edge of the Jawbone Canyon network of trails. The road dropped into the valley on the north end and cut straight along the middle of the valley before turning to the southeast, where it climbed a pass and disappeared beyond an array of wind turbines along the ridgeline. The road itself served many of the rural residents that dwelled in this far corner of the desert as they commuted to and from jobs in faraway towns, evidenced by the routine nature of car headlights I observed at night.

Once on the road, I followed it north and climbed the next mile to the pass where it intersected the Pacific Crest trail. The road turned from dirt to paved at exactly this point, as if to signal a threshold between the Wild West and the Just-Plain-Old West. Along the wide shoulder were caches of water for thru-hikers who often used the nearby Joshua trees as a shady rest stop in the middle of the day. I was surprised there were no hikers as I left the road and took the trail to the east, although I was thinking about how crazy thru-hikers must be to dedicate four months to walking, especially through these desert segments.

I pressed on—the mountain peak now looked only a few miles away, but most of the climbing was still ahead. I loped along the trail for half a mile before turning off onto a thin single-track. Cheatgrass and devil's fiddleneck covered the disturbed landscape. Fortunately, these plants were still soft and green. By late summer they would dry out, producing an excruciating thicket of spines and seeds. Once the trail disappeared, I continued onward, using my best judgment to ascend the rocky summit above. As the terrain became steeper and the path forward less obvious, I slowed to a slog. The vegetated hillside turned into a labyrinth of boulders and steep ravines, and I stopped frequently to consider the best route. After turning a corner around a large buttress, I startled a deer from its hideout. It disappeared down the hillside, blending effortlessly with the landscape. I stopped again for a moment and surveyed the terrain above. The most navigable route looked to take me under a large arch formed in the last band of broken cliffs that shielded the summit. I found my way through the final few hundred feet and navigated a maze of third-class scrambling to the summit of the peak.

Finally on top, I enjoyed a 360-degree panorama of the surrounding desert landscape and the cooling effect of up-slope mountain winds. Far to the northeast and through the thick desert air lay Ridgecrest and the naval base on China Lake. The desert surrounded the city in an endless sea of brown, disrupted occasionally by braided ribbons of green riparian habitat. To the south, the vast landscape was speckled with solar farms, the large rectangular shapes reflecting sunlight, visible from afar. I turned back to the west, where I had come from. Far below, I could barely make out the minuscule oak tree of our camp.

I found the radio in my pack. "Hey, Jason, can you hear me?" I said over the static and waited a few moments.

"Hello," he responded.

"Jason, look through your binoculars at the rocky peak to the east," I said. "Can you see me?" I flapped my arms like a madman.

"Hard to say," he said after a few moments. "It's still pretty far away-looking in my binoculars. Hey, kinda hot, isn't it?" he added, apparently concerned for my mental state.

"Oh, man. It was great. The path disappeared so I had to do a bit of trailblazing," I shouted into the radio. "I'll be back down there in a couple hours."

"Okay, have fun," he replied doubtfully and signed off.

Wind gusts whipped as I hobbled around the boulder-strewn peak looking for a summit register. Often in an old ammo can, you may be lucky enough to find a flask of whiskey tucked away alongside an assortment of other objects. Eventually, I found it stuffed in a crack, but unfortunately, no booze. Like a time capsule, the small notebook inside contained entries going back a quarter century. One pair of summiteers was from Mexico. "Caught in a thunderstorm," said another. As I thumbed through the wrinkled pages, I found my old friend Keith's name, printed years ago, in the '90s. *I was just a kid in Alabama,* I thought. I pulled the pencil stub from the bottom of the can and scribbled a message to the future.

I enjoyed a few more minutes of the vista before growing tired of the wind and beginning my descent. I followed, as best I could, the circuitous path I had climbed up. Looping around unnavigable terrain and avoiding dead-ends. Going down is generally faster than going up—so long as you don't miss a turn. Away from the windy summit, the heat of the day became overbearing. I had thought I would easily be back in a couple hours; now I wasn't so sure. I trudged along though, still enjoying the scenery. Ravens overhead. Flowers in bloom. Blue sky and the occasional lofty cloud floating overhead. But my tranquility was interrupted when I realized my water bottle was empty. "*Shit. Well, I can get more at the water caches by the trail junction,*" I reassured myself.

Trying to ignore my growing thirst, I eventually reached the road again and noticed several people milling around in whatever small patches of shade they could find. A dusty-looking bunch, many in long sleeves and sporting sun hats. A white truck was parked along the shoulder. My first thought was they were a group of birders or a natural history club. But, as I got closer, their blank stares and sun-bleached gear told me they were in fact PCT thru-hikers. But one of them, a rather well-fed and sane-looking man, was conspicuously out of place in the small group of sinewy, tanned bodies. He was in the process of unloading, in order of importance, beer, water, and soda.

"Hey there," he said enthusiastically from under his ball cap.

"Hi, how are y'all doin'?" I said as I stopped in the middle of the road. Surrounded by so many people all dealing with the midday heat, I became even more acutely aware of the suffocating temperature and brutal sunshine. I restrained myself from stumbling over and grabbing a drink from his hand.

The group of hikers looked tired and hungry and didn't say much. Over the years I had interacted with many a thru-hiker and was familiar with the shy nature that often develops after weeks of solitary existence in the wilderness. To further enhance this general introversion, the stretch of trail they were in was notoriously hot, dry, and devoid of water. All they really wanted at this point was a cold drink and a patch of shady real estate in which to enjoy it.

"Wait, were you just *running*?" called a hiker, seated under a Joshua tree. He sounded perplexed.

"Oh, just a bit of a run-walk up the mountain," I said as I pointed to the peak behind me. "What's goin' on here?" I asked, still very distracted by the thought of the nearby liquid.

"Well, I'm restocking the trail cache here," said the well-nourished man as he turned from his truck bed with a cooler full of drinks on ice. My throat constricted.

"A trail angel!" I exclaimed. "I've always wanted to see one. You from Weldon?"

"No. Ridgecrest," he replied with a smile. "You want something cold to drink?" Like a wizard conjuring a potion, he waved his arm over the cooler. "*I thought you'd never ask,*" my brain retorted.

"Oh man, do I," I said out loud. "The beer looks great, but I ran out of water and should hydrate first."

His hand disappeared briefly into the cooler before reappearing with an ice-cold water. The bottle felt surreal in my hand, like an elixir materializing from a daydream.

"Thank you," I replied before taking a long gulp. The cold liquid hurt as it hit my parched throat.

"What are you doing here?" he asked as he continued to unload his truck.

"I'm doing field work. Down in the valley." I pointed toward the general vicinity of my camp. "I was too hot to sleep anymore, and I got restless. Decided to go for a little outing." I smiled.

"That's crazy," the hiker under the Joshua tree piped up again. "Middle of the day! It's fuckin' hot!"

"Yeah, well, I work all night and try to sleep as much I can in the mornings. I guess I went a little crazy," I explained. But inside my head I was thinking how crazy *he* was. Spending four to five months in essentially solitary existence doing the same thing almost every day—walking. Now, to be fair, the thru-hiker scene becomes a well-developed community each year. But they are out there! For a long time. That's *crazy*. I don't think I would have the focus. But I WAS out jogging in the middle of the day. That's *crazy*.

The trail angel lifted the cooler and began carrying it down the trail. "I keep the cooler a few hundred feet off the road, near the trail register," he said. "Feel free to help yourself."

The hikers all seemed settled into the afternoon heat and were quiet. They would spend the remaining daylight hours napping in whatever shade they could find before setting off on the trail again at nightfall. I decided I should get back to camp myself.

"Well, y'all enjoy the afternoon," I said. "I need to get back."

"You enjoy yourself too," hollered the angel with a nod of his head.

The others waved as I trotted back into the valley. In the heat, I plodded along, thinking to myself about the absurdity of the afternoon. There I was, running in the middle of the day. I meet thru-hikers. They think I'm crazy. I think they're crazy. Hell, maybe even the trail angel is crazy for giving away drinks to strangers. In the end, I suspect we're all crazy.

Back at camp, the others were gone, likely exploring the shadows of nearby canyons. The beer cooler was in full sun. I scanned the surroundings and moved it into the shade of a small shrub. I pulled out a beer—luckily still cold—then moved my chair into another patch of shade, sat down, and took off my shoes. Leaning back, I dug my bare toes into the cool sand and enjoyed the beverage.

What Remains in a Land
of Diminishing Returns

I CHECKED the final trap then tipped the last drops of cold coffee into my mouth. The trapline followed a belt of creosote and desert almond shrubs and ended at the edge of a dry channel. I sat and dangled my legs over the incised bank of the wash where plant roots and stones pierced the vertical layers of exposed soil. Below, braids of silt and sand mixed with cobbles and trash. Evidence of the ephemeral waters that had woven this tapestry of color and texture. Small green herbs of spring were emerging. Unselfish, these wildflowers needed only water enough to grow for a season, then wither and die.

I savored the solitude for a few minutes before starting back to the truck. It was only 9 a.m., and I had spent most of the last two days in Pine Tree Canyon. I needed a break from the incessant gunfire that would resume by midday, and I wanted to explore some local points of interest in Fremont Valley. At some point, I also needed to get to a store, so I packed some snacks and drove into the valley below.

My first destination was a historical marker at a place called Desert Spring, somewhere near Cantil, a small community of rundown ranch homes and abandoned farming equipment surrounded by a sea of salt bush and other desert plants. After following a convoluted route of two-lane roads and some navigational bungling, I found the location. I parked under the shade of a dying tree and stepped from my truck. A cool breeze rattled leaves, and the pungent odor of desert plants met my nose. I took a long breath and wished I could spend more time in the desert during the cooler winter months.

I followed a ramshackle fence line a few hundred meters until it disappeared. The monument was not much more than an agglomeration of multi-colored desert stones, and it stood among the dried remains of shrubs lying prostrate on the desert sand. A metallic plaque mortared in the center was inscribed with a brief description of the historical significance of the spring. It once sustained Native Americans and nourished bumbling European prospectors in search of riches. Now it was little more than a specter of the past. A parched ruin. A monument to the collective exploitation of the environment from generations of eager settlers chasing Manifest Destiny and the American Dream. The scarce waters that once fed this land had been tapped into long ago and taken away—Los Angeles had an insatiable appetite for the lifeblood of these desert valleys. The only plants and animals that endured here were those that survive on little rainfall or what moisture they could extract from the food they ate. Lizards eyed me from atop splintered wooden fenceposts as I plodded through fine sand back to the truck. I sat in the cab and drank lukewarm water from my bottle before pulling back onto the road toward Highway 14 and Mojave—the small town that many from LA pass by without pause on their way north to Mammoth and the wilds of the Sierra Nevada.

The sheet metal of hangars and the bodies of aircraft glinted in the sunlight. An airport. A large and mysterious facility on the edge of town. I had read about this place but had only seen it from a distance. Here, the expansive desert was well suited for the Mojave Air and Space Port.

Originally a pair of dirt runways serving nearby mining operations, the airfield had evolved over many years into the behemoth facility it now was. During World War II, the federal government invested heavily in converting this rural airport into a training ground for the Air Force. The US military needed someplace to sharpen its lethal craft. And what better place to blow shit up than the middle of the desert? Eventually, the War Machine moved on to greener pastures and left the facility in public hands. The vacated airfield, all three thousand acres of it, became a blank canvas for the eclectic manifestations of US consumerism and world dominance. It now hosted a variety of enterprises, from an aircraft boneyard, where retired airliners desiccate under the relentless desert sun, to a space port, where the restless patriarchy ejaculates its metallic dreams into Earth's orbit.

As I neared the turn onto Airport Boulevard, giant aircraft loomed over the intersection, inviting tourists. The tree-lined road ended after a mile in a maze of gated driveways, hangars, and a park. Signs pointed directions to several firms that had taken up residence. From testing to manufacturing, the campus was now home to a variety of private sector companies invested in space exploration.

I parked near The Voyager restaurant and walked across the pavement toward Legacy Park. The small square boasted an assortment of memorabilia representing the area's history. A model mine shaft and cart commemorated the days when the airport served the nearby mining industry. In the middle of the park stood a large rocket. The giant cone was a failed project of a failed company, but an inscription at the base prompted observers to never give up on one's dreams. Inside a small building, a replica of the SpaceShipOne craft sat behind large glass windows. Unlike the failed rocket outside, this artifact of unrelenting human perseverance was worth protecting from the elements. Unlike the failed rocket outside, this symbolized the human triumph in space.

Other than the park, there didn't seem much else to do, and I wandered aimlessly. A security guard snoozed in his idling truck. The restaurant was closed, and the only buildings that looked interesting were off-limits to the public. I walked back to my truck and drove several miles along trash-lined fences to the far end of the airport. Along the northern boundary, I came upon a viewpoint over the airplane boneyard. In a sea of metal, retired airliners slowly, imperceptibly, returned to dust. With rare rainfall and perennially low humidity, the area's climate is the perfect place to ignore these mechanical behemoths. They had served their country and contributed their part to the free market. Picked clean of parts, skeletons now lie in their final resting place.

Despite the apparent investments by the techno-industrial complex, Mojave, like many small desert towns within LA's sphere of influence, embodied neglect. As I approached the main highway heading back into town, wiry men rode bicycles along the shoulder. Bags draped over their handlebars. I passed abandoned store fronts with cracked windows. A billboard cautioned: "Syphilis, A Silent Killer."

To say this desert outpost had a drug problem would be to point out the painfully obvious. And I don't mean lazy locals malingering under clouds of marijuana smoke. Pot was, after all, now lawful in California, and many rural municipalities rushed to cater to the industry. Adelanto, about an hour to the southeast, was an example—from seed to herb-infused chocolate edible, this former orchard town had turned to weed for economic prosperity. With the endorsed monetization of reefer, the bureaucracy that once incarcerated derelicts for possession had happily parted with its self-appointed morals. But even so, outlaws, hell-bent on peddling pot to states where it remained illegal, operated throughout the desert. Drug cartels pilfered ground water to cultivate black-market crops, leaving a scourge of environmental disaster in their wake. But problems of weed aside, Mojave suffered from meth addiction, by both users and manufacturers. Miles of isolated desert and abandoned settlements rendered the area ideal for production of the sinister drug. And its proximity to LA and Vegas were ideal for distribution. In the epicenter of the Kern County meth corridor, roughly half of all felonies were associated with the drug. In this land of raw beauty, peace officers were engaged in a never-ending battle with the unsanctioned ravages of tweakers and vile criminals.

I once shared a beer with a pair of estate sale hunters in the area. After scoring high-dollar items, they sold them at a storefront in town. Often, their inventory consisted of heirlooms that had reached the end of their familial life span, one way or another. On this sunny day, the hunters made off with a set of lucrative 19th-century porcelain china that had descended a chain of custody for several generations inside the walls of a quaint family home. Unfortunately, that chain ended when the present owner, who had a full-time job several hours away, rented the place out. Apparently with little scrutiny of the renters. Unbeknownst to the poor woman, she had left her family home to a posse of meth heads. After several months away, she returned to chaos. The interior was destroyed; doors had been ripped from their hinges and used for firewood in the winter. Her dog, which the tenants were supposed to feed, was dead in the yard. When the cops hauled the clan away, little was left. The house, a teardown. But somehow the porcelain survived. And after some polishing and an appraisal, it would tantalize window shoppers from a display case. In a bizarre rendering, these family heirlooms, recovered and sold for a profit, were the recycled shards of an American Dream lost to a nightmare.

I navigated the city streets toward the grocery store. Amid shuttered businesses and unoccupied buildings were occasional coffee shops and delicatessens. Colorful signs aroused salivary glands and promised "The Best Around." People strolled the cracked sidewalks and waved at one another. Crossing guards helped school children across the road. There was more here than junkies with pock-marked faces and bad habits. Here, just like anywhere else, were people in a resolute struggle to carve out a living. In this harsh and beautiful desert of diminishing resources, the good life may still exist. If only for a chosen few, and perhaps for only a time.

I pulled into the Stater Bros. lot and parked my truck. A passing freight train sent shock waves through the earth. Plastic bags and soda cups danced across the pavement in a dry breeze. Other than the grocery store, the strip mall was a collection of vacant establishments. A shutdown library. An old doctor's office. One large building standing alone was once a non-denominational church: "Open Heaven Worship Center." A leathery panhandler sat at the curb holding a sign, "Anything helps. God Bless."

Regrettably, my first order of business was computer work. With a warm breeze passing through open windows, I sat in my truck and checked emails, downloaded data, and perused my calendar for the coming months of summer. Two trips to the field from Reno: cumulative 1200 miles. A trip to Utah to see family: 1100 miles. Flying to D.C. for the Mammalogy meeting: 5000 miles round trip. *"Jesus Christ,"* I thought to myself. *"What kind of environmentally conscious ecologist am I? I'm no better than a desert sod farmer!"* I was traveling most of the summer and would likely consume as many resources in three months as a Gilded Age tycoon of the 19th century could in a whole year. And I was just a desert rat trying to make an honest living out of the back of my truck.

I gathered my wits, extracted myself from the truck, and started across the parking lot to the store to get a few supplies before heading back out into the field. *"Maybe a bottle of rye too,"* I thought.

"Excuse me, sir?" a girl's voice said from behind me. "Would you like to buy some tamales?" She spoke urgently and walked toward me and away from a green minivan. An older woman sat in the driver's seat and a man leaned on the back with the cooler full of tamales.

"Sorry, I don't have any cash," I replied.

She turned without comment and walked toward a family that was unloading from their Tesla parked at a charging station. I continued into the store and walked straight to the restrooms. As I approached, a slender woman escorted a young child and an older man into one of the two private restrooms. The man, apparently autistic, self-soothed as he entered.

I too felt in need of some relief when I stepped into the open restroom and found a pool of vomit in front of the toilet. The sour smell burned my nostrils, and I finished my business quickly and walked out. A boy sporting a store uniform and a grave facial expression hurriedly pushed a mop bucket toward the toilets.

I quickly found bananas, an avocado, and a bottle of rye whiskey. After some sleuthing, I liberated a dusty green bottle of propane from an obscure shelf between the front doors and the magazine rack. A man in a camo T-shirt and denims perused the latest issue of *Guns and Ammo*. At the checkout line, I remembered the family selling tamales in the parking lot, so I asked for two twenties.

Outside however, the family was nowhere to be found. After searching for a few minutes, I gave up. I knew the reality. The girl had been in a hurry when she asked me to buy tamales. They had to move quickly, sell as much as they could, and get out before drawing too much notice. Undocumented immigrants can't risk much attention. Especially now, "America First" means everyone else takes a back seat. We get first dibs, and everyone else gets to fight over scraps. But hell, maybe that's always been the case.

As I got into my truck, a strung-out redneck was shouting obscenities into the open door of a nearby van. "Fuck you, bitch. I ain't gone to all this work for nothing!" He backed away, and a woman, also shouting, pursued him to a Chevy pickup. Their shouting reached a crescendo as they climbed into the truck. The motor strained to start before the man gunned the engine. With tires screeching, they accelerated away before suddenly stopping. Out of the side window shot a bag of fast food. French fries and hamburger leftovers landed on the asphalt. A smorgasbord for grackles lurking in the nearby trees. The truck peeled out and sped off down the highway.

I was glad to leave town and head back into the canyon for the night. As I drove up Highway 14, jet contrails left thin arcs of white clouds across the blue sky. Windmills along the hills to the west moved lazily in a gentle breeze. Farther up the road, solar farms cut through the desert, reflecting the afternoon sun. I slowed down as I approached Pine Tree Canyon and turned onto the dirt road that meandered west. Shortly after the turn was a sign marked "LADWP Pine Tree Canyon Project." And then a cautionary sign: "Slow. Tortoise Zone."

I drove slowly with the windows down to enjoy the pleasant weather. It was only in the 60s, and the sun was out. A few trucks with attached trailers were parked along the dirt road. ATV folks were somewhere in the distant hills, enjoying miles of open and dusty roads. The silence was punctuated occasionally by the blast of gunfire or the roar of an F/A-18 overhead. The mark of human presence was all around, from wind farms to shell casings left scattered along the desert floor. But still, there was beauty left in this abused landscape.

The road passed under the smaller of two LA Department of Water and Power aqueducts. In a classic "use-it-or-lose-it" scenario, this white pipe was built after the original aqueduct when LADWP discovered that it was not exporting its maximum allotment of water through the first pipeline. Who knows who made that discovery? Perhaps an enthusiastic and underpaid intern, hoping to leave a mark and land a big job. Regardless, it meant LA could really suck these desert valleys dry. To hell with 'em.

Not far beyond, tucked around the next ridge, was the original LADWP aqueduct. The pipeline dropped down into the canyon from the north and then rose steeply on the other side until it disappeared into the mountainside. Pure gravity and simple plumbing carried the water down and back up again. Ten feet in diameter, the tube looked almost insignificant in the vast surroundings. Almost too small to carry away the whole of the Owens River. The river that had fed innumerable wetlands, irrigated countless ranches, and filled Owens Lake was now carried off to quench the ever-growing thirst of Southern California. It was hard to believe that LADWP's annual budget contained millions of dollars to maintain this long straw. The imposing piece of engineering traveled over two hundred miles, up and down mountains. A demonstration of the hubris of humankind. And the amount of money spent annually on this beige tube, dwarfed in the surrounding landscape, was a testament to the value of water in the American West.

The road crossed this larger pipeline, and as I crested the top of the bridge, I saw several people target shooting along the far end of the dry channel. *"What keeps them from shooting the damn pipeline?"* I thought. I drove through the wash as jackrabbits sprinted across the road.

My camp sat along the north side of the canyon a half mile farther. Old fire pits were scattered around. Trash stuck to the base of shrubs. Shotgun shells, bullet casings, blasted pieces of clay pigeons. Shards of glass. But I enjoyed the little bit of nature encircling my truck. A creosote bush offered its aroma. A bat hunted above my truck for insects. I unfolded my camp chair and sat down to enjoy the marigold colors of sunset as the last of the gunfire echoed from the canyon walls.

"Humans are *slobs",* I thought. The whole lot of us. The rednecks up here in the desert shoot shit. Living, inanimate, it makes little difference to them. Many don't clean up after themselves either. And the responsible ones can't shake the stereotype. To educated city folk, they're all a bunch of yokels. But what is this land to the elite? A place to protect, sure. People like to contribute to things they care about. And there is no shortage of wealthy urbanites who enjoy shelling out a few bucks for a worthy cause. Maybe they even visit the hinterlands on occasion. Escape the reverberations of the city for the simplicity of the desert. Perhaps, we're all complicit in these insidious acts perpetrated upon our shared Mother Earth.

The setting sun cast a glow upon the pipeline that climbed so steeply up the side of the canyon. The long straw. Protecting the water from this harsh and arid land as it traveled to Southern California. Apparently where it was needed more. Water for the millions who lived there. Water for food. Water for drinking. Water for cleaning. For the hospitals. Churches. Universities. Water for golf courses, and lawns, and fountains erected as monuments to the restless madmen who carved out the desert to create the improbable oasis that is now Southern California. Somehow there would always be more water.

I turned to the east and watched the cloudless sky transform from pastel hues of blue and purple to darkness. The peaks of jagged mountains formed silhouettes on the fading horizon. Somewhere upcanyon, coyotes yapped at the coming nightfall. I thought of the Mexican family selling homemade tamales. In a hurry. Rushing off to set up someplace else. They only wanted what all of us want. Was there any left?

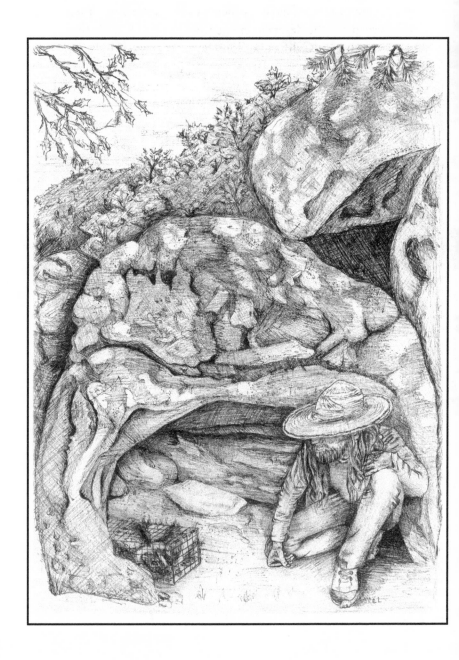

Getting Skunked

GETTING SKUNKED has become a common figure of speech. *Jimmy and I went fishin' this mornin' and got skunked. You see the game last night? Cougars got skunked.* It's a fun expression, except when it happens to you. Especially literally.

I woke from a restful night's slumber. A corner spot at Chico Flat campground, with the white noise of the nearby Kern River, made for ideal sleeping conditions. I climbed out of the sleeping pod that was the back of my truck and stretched. The sun was still below the ridgeline to the east, and its rays were just beginning to illuminate the topmost portion of the western rim. The smell of wildfire smoke accompanied a thick haze that made everything look farther away. I was about 10 minutes upstream from Kernville, and the morning highway traffic hummed with trucks pulling trailers full of whitewater rafts for a day on the river. I set some water to boil for coffee and walked my empties from the previous night to a nearby dumpster. Recycling may have been the better option, but I had seen many a desert-dwelling vagrant benefit from salvaging recyclables from dumpsters, and I was ok with that.

"*Besides,*" I thought to myself. "*Isn't most of our recycling just sent back to China in otherwise empty shipping containers? They probably just use what they can and toss the rest back in the ocean where it eventually ends up swirling in that giant vortex somewhere in the middle of the Pacific Ocean. Goddam. I should just fill growlers.*"

The water had come to a boil, and I poured the steaming liquid into the French press and watched the thick brown mixture as it bubbled. I rummaged through my cookware and found a mug with residue of red wine on the bottom. I rinsed it with what was left of the hot water. It wasn't perfect but good enough for the company I kept.

While the coffee brewed, I walked down the cobbly hillside to the river's edge. The mighty Kern River was crooned about by the late, great Merle Haggard, country legend and gift to this world from the oft-disparaged city of Bakersfield, California. Though rich in arts and culture, and having produced and inspired generations of great musicians, Bakersfield has earned the tagline "The Armpit of California." Years of resource exploitation and agricultural overuse have taken their toll on the city. Gang violence, pollution, and drugs filled the void that was left after the spoils of the American Dream had been looted by the greedy.

I walked back to the truck and poured a cup of syrupy black coffee. I checked the time. "*Seven-thirty, time to go check the traplines.*" As much as I would enjoy some alone time in the hills, I came in search of woodrats.

Woodrats, pack rats, trade rats are all common names for the medium-sized rodents that belong to the genus *Neotoma* and live throughout the United States. To many, they are vermin. Builders of nests in the most inconvenient places, from garages to car engines. But these small mammals have much to teach us. They carefully construct their stick nests and adorn them with curious objects they find in their environment. Bones, sticks, and rocks are among the natural tchotchkes they like to use. In our modern landscapes, beer cans, shell casings, and shiny Mylar balloons can be found delicately placed throughout their stick-built homes. Woodrats also maintain a sense of personal hygiene, perhaps better than many humans. For anyone who has owned a pet rodent, it will come as no surprise that woodrats produce a prolific amount of poop. They organize their excrement in latrines, which can accumulate over many generations. Woodrats mostly live alone in their cozy homes, except for mothers with pups, but they pass them down from one generation to the next. This produces layer upon layer of historical artifacts, a record of natural history for anyone inclined to interpret the clues. Scientists study ancient packrat middens because, like time capsules, the layers of objects and feces provide insights into the history of an area.

I was particularly interested in the local population of woodrats for my research on diet-related adaptations. Woodrats are primarily herbivores and consume a variety of plants, some of which are highly toxic. I had a hunch that this population may consume, among a variety of other plants, California coffeeberry, which naturally produces a laxative effect. Parts of the plant have been used therapeutically by Indigenous people for thousands of years. Great if you are stopped up, but overdosing on these plants could be harmful to a desert rodent. Thanks to modern DNA sequencing technology, all I needed was a pile of fresh poop to identify the plants eaten by woodrats here.

I hopped in my truck and drove up around the next bend. Still safely in the shade, my trapline meandered along the base of a wooded hillside. The day before I had seen plenty of woodrat nests with fresh sign of activity, so I knew they were here. I slowly walked the line, closing empty traps as I went. Unfortunately, ants had carried off much of the bait I had used.

I would add more when I opened them again in the evening, once the heat of midday was past.

"Nineteen of 20. Nothing yet," I thought. The last pair of traps were placed under a large boulder beneath an oak tree. I clambered up the hill and ducked under branches, avoiding poison oak along the way. As I approached a trap near the opening to a small cave at the base of the boulder, I began to recoil instinctively. At first, unsure why. Then, horribly sure.

"Holy shit, it's a skunk." I winced. White and black glossy hair protruded from the wire sides of the fully closed trap. It pierced my soul with its blank gaze. *"Why?! Goddamn you!!!"* I reached my arms up to the sky like a prophet and cried out— much more softly than I wanted to, as to not agitate the ungodly hell beast. I had been spoiled by the relative simplicity of rat trapping at my arid desert sites, where skunks are rare.

"Jesus Christ, what should I do?" I thought miserably to myself. *"I'll just go back to the truck. Yeah, I have that bottle of whiskey. I'll just go back and drink some whiskey. No, you asshat, it's barely eight in the morning. Think."*

I stood quietly, now locked in a staring contest with the trapped skunk. After a moment, I realized I didn't smell the skunk, which meant it hadn't covered everything within 15 feet with its foul stench. Yet. I watched it a little longer. It appeared angry, but stable. I thought some more and began to construct a kind of plan as I backed slowly away and walked back to my truck.

I groped through a plastic bin of supplies and found a roll of 13-gallon trash bags. I took one and slowly walked back to the unwanted prisoner. I remembered a discussion with administrators at my university about what I would do if I captured a skunk, as if I should have a formal standard operating procedure in place for such an unlikely event. What the hell would I do? Didn't know, didn't care. It had seemed pretty speculative at the time. Well, now I guess I would find out.

I wasn't sure exactly what I would do, but half-baked ideas are common when doing field work. The natural world doesn't provide the predictability that modern living has imposed on humanity. Holding the large trash bag, I stood staring at the skunk. It noticed me. It seemed angry. But still no spray. I found two sticks, each about two feet long, and used them to hold the trash bag out in front of me, providing a barrier between me and the ticking stink bomb. Moving slowly and with the focus of a bomb-squad technician, I placed the bag over the trap. Now I at least had a thin layer of protection, which might also help calm the skunk.

"Well, I still have a skunk in a trap. What now?" I thought. I had to open the trap door to let the skunk out. But it was standing on the mechanism that had triggered the door to shut. I could open the door but would have to physically hold it open until the skunk walked out. No way in hell was I gonna sit mere inches away from the ass end of a skunk and take a blast to the face.

I backed away to a safe distance and pondered the situation. Still no smell, so I knew I hadn't lost the battle yet. I found another small stick, maybe six inches long, and thick enough to have some structural integrity. I slowly edged back over to the trap, acutely aware of the skunk within, and kneeled. I slowly inched the trap door open with one hand and grasped the stick with the other. Sweat began beading on my forehead as flies buzzed overhead. I held my breath. Furtively but without hesitation, I placed one end of the stick under the trap door and angled the other end into the moist soil. The stick was just long enough to hold the door open all the way, and just strong enough to keep it that way. I slowly scooted away to a safe distance and watched for a moment to see if the crackpot apparatus would stay put. When no collapse and ensuing stink Armageddon seemed imminent, I let out a deep breath and walked back to the truck.

Very wide awake, I finished my cup of now cold coffee and considered again opening the bottle of whiskey. Instead, I passed another 10 minutes on a nearby rock and listened to birds singing in the tree branches above. The morning chorus was mostly over, but the sparrows and finches apparently still had a few things to tell the world. An occasional car passed by on the nearby road, but traffic had slowed considerably. The river rats were enjoying the water by now. A narrow highway of ants moved in synchrony along the sparsely vegetated ground, heading toward one of my traps. They would harvest what bits of bait remained for their underground colony.

"Am I like one of these ants?" I thought. *"Here I am doing field work for my research as a graduate student. I like what I do and made the choice to do what I do. And I love the field work too, current excitement notwithstanding. But, back at the university, I am a small cog in the giant machine of progress. If I'm honest with myself, the isolation of field work I once longed for now brings me a level of anxiety. How many emails will I have when I get back to an internet connection? How much more work will I have to do to fulfill the ever-growing demands of granting agencies, and university administrators? Growth, they say. Increase student enrollment, they say. More warm bodies in classrooms means more money for the university. More research grants mean more money for the university. Growth, growth, growth, they say. In all my classes in ecology and conservation biology, unchecked growth is often at the core of many of the problems we are concerned about."*

After these cynical thoughts, I slowly walked back to my ludicrous experiment. On approach, there was no smell. Good sign. I slowly crouched to peek under the boulder. The trap was still covered so I couldn't see if the skunk was inside, but the door was still open. After a moment my eyes adjusted, and I spotted the unmistakable markings of the striped skunk out of the trap and in the back of the cave. Black with two white stripes running along either side of its back, and one thin stripe through the center of its head. It stared back at me as I carefully unhooked the stick, eased down the trap door, and slid the contraption backwards. As I backed away, the skunk walked deeper in the cave, occasionally glaring back at me.

A warm sense of relief grew in my chest, and I felt dizzy as I stood to walk back to the truck. I collected my supplies and drove to camp which now lay bare to the sun. I found the bottle of whiskey and splashed a bit into my cup, then found a patch of shade for my chair and sat down with a huge sigh.

Suddenly, an electronic *ping* pierced the anticipated tranquility. Unfortunately, a cellular signal must have found its way up the canyon just long enough to alert my phone of a new email. I was afraid to look. My friend had once lost a receipt during an exceptionally long field stint in an exceptionally remote locality. Months later, he received an email informing him of a missing receipt in the amount of $3.28 for a purchase made some several months prior. "Previous correspondences regarding the delinquent receipt have been ignored," it read. After some poking around, he discovered the initial email had been sent to an email address he was not aware he had. Apparently, the bureaucrats in the accounting office had established an email account for him, without telling him, expressly for the purpose of informing him of his negligence in handling receipts. Eventually he was informed, "The $3.28 has been applied to another account, which your funds will have to reimburse." Without checking the message, I turned the phone off and tossed it into my truck. Whatever absurdity waited for me in the outside world, it could wait.

"What a morning," I said out loud. One skunk and not a single woodrat. I guess I got skunked. I sat back, closed my eyes, and listened to the words of Merle Haggard in my mind as the Kern River played its perennial refrain.

Straight Flossin'
___ Along the Great Western Frontier ___

CASSIDY AND I had been driving north on Highway 395 all morning. From the deserts of Nevada to the forests of the Northwest and on to Portland, in one well-tuned, 10-hour stretch. We started the day listening to classic country, then kept our minds busy with The Dead as we rolled into southern Oregon. As a hiatus from our nomadic days of rambling through the desert, we had left our solitude to attend the annual meeting of the Ecological Society of America. The weeklong meeting would provide opportunities to rub shoulders with influential figures in the field. And it was in the Rose City, a mecca of progressive ideals. We pursued the event with an idealism not yet suffocated by the irrationality of institutional bureaucracy. In a world of increasingly chaotic ecological disasters, we were inspired by such a meeting of the minds. Constantly floating in a sea of questions, we hoped to find answers. If we could survive.

On this hot August day, the great Western Frontier was thoroughly ablaze. Like a strange carnival, the tents of wildfire base camps lined the sides of the highway, headquarters for the thousands of personnel battling the flames of Manifest Destiny. In northeastern California, we had no luck getting even a glimpse of Mount Shasta. The snow-capped volcanic peak I remembered from family road trips during my childhood was hidden somewhere in the opaque miasma.

Cassidy paused from belting out a verse from Wharf Rat. "That's wildfire season for ya," he said.

"I wonder how many of these fires are started by assholes flicking cigarette butts out their car windows," I said. Somehow, in the bleakness of the burned-out West, I wanted to smoke, so I rooted through bags in the back seat for a pouch of tobacco. I came up empty but, in the quest, found my flask and drank what drops of whiskey remained before settling back into my seat and watching the landscape pass by. The entire region was a poster child for the consequences of the arrogance of a single species. Whole stands of evergreen forest dead from years of drought and beetle infestation. Burn scars along mountainsides, still stained orange from retardant used to put out previous fires. Chemical residues that may remain in the ecosystem for years, propagating other disasters, some not yet fully understood. Perhaps the focal point of some future ecology student's dissertation.

We continued our passage into southern Oregon. Evergreen trees, dead and alive, filled the landscape. Here and there communities were stamped into the sea of green biomass like the work of some giant cookie cutter. Lifted trucks, sporting NRA bumper stickers, reminded me that Oregon was more than its progressive urban centers. The sweeping deserts of eastern Oregon and the rural lumber towns were still home to a populace invested in ranching, timber, and other vocational trades. Industries that had fueled the American Dream of a bygone era now struggled to survive in the new world.

We arrived at the town of Chemult, a rural community off Highway 97. Cassidy pulled into a gas station, and I hopped out before I remembered you don't pump your own gas in Oregon.

"Oh right. Just fill it with regular," I told the dutiful pump attendant who greeted me.

We were also starving. But a Chicken Torpedo from the gas station didn't sound appetizing. I eyed the ubiquitous Subway and shook my head.

"We should support local," I said.

"Hell, yeah," Cassidy replied. "Fuck Subway."

Once a rail station town, Chemult now seemed to have more closed businesses than people. A few gas stations, a handful of roadside motor lodges, and various convenience stores were surrounded by vacated buildings in assorted stages of dereliction.

After being hoodwinked by several diners that we had hoped would harbor a juicy burger or a piece of homemade pie, our hopes began to fade. KJ's Café down the road had strange hours posted on the door, and, after pressing my face against the front door window, I lost all confidence that it was even still in business. Cassidy spotted a small deli up the road, and we decided to stretch our legs. We walked by a broken-down RV in an empty dirt lot, its gas door flap open. A hopeless-looking fellow with greasy hair sat next to it in a rocking chair. He stared at his flip phone while sipping a Bud Light. Everywhere smelled of diesel smoke and burning brake pads. Trucks, loaded down with timber, barreled along the highway. As if it knew the jig was up, the logging industry frantically extracted what was left before it all burned to the ground.

We reached the deli that doubled as a gas station. An old gentleman with a ball cap and a dignified demeanor stood next to his Chevy truck, waiting for gas. Inside, a colorful menu board lit up the interior of what looked like a one-size-fits-all establishment. Up front had the usual gas station wares—snacks, cold drinks, vehicle maintenance fluids, and a rack of smutty magazines for the lonely road tripper. We wandered to the back and rang the bell.

"I dunno, not too promising," Cassidy said. "I suppose it's a one-man show here."

"Shouldn't there be a cute daughter to help?" I said.

"I'm sure they've all left for the big city. Find their true calling," Cassidy said with a smile.

We waited a few minutes, hopeful because the boysenberry shakes looked good, and the chicken sandwich was only five bucks. Finally, we stepped back outside and found the elderly man still standing patiently by his truck, methodically packing dip into his lower lip.

"Hey, there," I said. "You know where the owner is?"

"Yeah." His voice was muffled. "He's open, just he's helpin' fill them tanks over there with that fella." He pointed toward two men standing languidly by a large propane tank.

"Oh, I see," I said. "Well, thanks." I nodded to the man as he leaned back against his truck.

Reluctantly, Cassidy and I cut our losses and set our eyes on the Double D Mountain Market across the road. The market promised, among other gastronomic delights, chicken, pizza, and liquor.

We crossed the highway, dodging semis and the occasional well-polished classic car headed south for Hot August Nights—Reno's annual event that rejoiced in America's love affair with cars and rock 'n' roll. Just inside was an aisle dedicated to the liquor. Mostly bottom-shelf varieties, but something for everyone. But we needed food, and we walked to the front to inquire about the fried chicken.

"Well, I'm about out of chicken tenders," said the nice gal, holding up a bag of a half-dozen quarter-sized pieces of what looked like frozen breadcrumbs. "I'll cook 'em all up and charge you for three pieces. How's that sound?"

"It's a steal," I said. "We'll take some potato wedges too."

"You got it," she replied and dunked the items in the deep fryer.

I grabbed a bottle of rum while Cassidy scrutinized the selection of Doritos.

"Don't forget ice," he said.

We darted back across the highway to the truck. After inhaling a few pieces of what-was-maybe chicken, a potato wedge, and burning my mouth in the process, I took the wheel, and we were off again. We ate our hard-won food as we passed miles in quiet solitude. The forest landscape was occasionally punctuated by buildings or old rail stations. These relics of human enterprise were slowly returning to nature over timescales unfathomable to most people.

Cassidy broke the silence as we wound through a mountainous stretch. "Ah, the PCT." He had walked the Pacific Crest Trail years before. He stared out the window in a spell of nostalgia. "I remember passing this point back in '06," he said.

Oh yeah," I said. "How long did it take you to get here from Tahoe?"

"I think about five or six weeks," he said. "But all of Oregon took only about three weeks. It goes fast. Compared to California, the Oregon section is short. And flat." He gazed out the window.

"Yeah, well, we just polished it off in half a day," I said. *"Time is strange,"* I thought. *"It's all relative. Maybe everything is relative."*

We followed Highway 58 over the pass toward Willamette Valley. The speed limit in Oregon seemed to max out at 55 miles per hour, so I tried to keep it under 80. When we got jammed up behind an 18-wheeler or one of the many varieties of rental RVs, I had to be patient and wait for a wide shoulder or passing lane.

You have to be careful around RVs on the open road. You never know if the person behind the wheel is an experienced veteran or an unfortunate renter who's been swindled by those looking to make a quick buck. You better remain vigilant around the latter. All too often, the driver has no clue—about large vehicles, narrow mountain roads, speed, and gravity. Most of my experience with rental RVs came from years of working and traveling around Yosemite National Park. Burned-out families trying to maintain the façade of happiness in the Great American West. Or a young couple taking a test drive in Vanlife. Once on the narrow and serpentine mountain roads, the poor wretches, white knuckles glued to the steering wheel, find themselves in the middle of a self-inflicted nightmare. I once watched two passing RVs sideswipe their mirrors, scattering glass and plastic all over the highway. I've heard rental insurance doesn't even cover this common occurrence.

We stopped along I-5 near Salem, about an hour south of Portland, to refuel and stretch our legs. The logging trucks and oversized pickups of the rural mountain roads with which camper vans had to contend were replaced by sedans and electric cars.

"Look at this," I said to Cassidy as an unwieldy RV careened into the parking. As it pulled alongside the gas pumps, a teenage bolted from the still-moving vehicle and disappeared behind the building. On the side of the monstrosity, "800-RV4RENT" was printed in bold letters. "Cruise America" was written across the back. The marketing experts had even thought to include an image of a dog looking out the side door. And all over the body of the vehicle were beautiful color pictures, in high-definition, of exploited hallmarks of the American West: Zion,

Yosemite, Yellowstone. A moving advertisement for the vanity of American consumerism. Whatever splendor existed in the natural world, grifters lurked nearby, waiting to wet their beaks.

"Jesus," Cassidy replied hopelessly, staring at the RV as he screwed the gas cap back on. "Well, we're all good to go," he added.

We crammed ourselves in the truck once more and set off for Portland. Visibility still piss-poor. Somewhere in the haze were the beautiful snow-capped volcanic peaks of the Cascade Range.

"Every time I visit Portland, I feel like it's become more of a caricature of itself," Cassidy said. We had entered the outskirts.

"Yeah, right," I said. "Portland has become its own parody." I looked out the window and surveyed the rush hour traffic. Thoroughly modern cars, whizzing around in a thoroughly modern city.

"It's so *cool* to be in Portland now," he went on in a biting tone. "Organic coffee, craft breweries, microbreweries, nanobreweries. Hell, probably even picobreweries now. Aquaponics too, let's not forget those." He listed off quirks that the world had come to associate with Portland.

We navigated to our motel. As poor graduate students on a budget, we were quickly priced out of the lavish rooms reserved for conference goers. Instead, I'd booked us a room at a Motel 6. It had received less than ideal reviews, but the price was right.

"It's coming up on the right," I said. "Ah, up there, just across from the Taco Bell and that strip-joint-looking place."

"Got it." Cassidy shifted into third gear as he moved over a couple lanes to turn into the parking lot of the rundown inn. In front of the office, two cops badgered a junky—a young fellow wearing shorts and a tank-top. He looked like he'd been strung out for a few days and just needed a meal.

"Uhhh, is that a prostitute over there?" Cassidy said as he pulled into an empty parking spot. A woman in a short red skirt stood in a corner of the lot. A cigarette hung loosely from her mouth. Her face was framed by wavy brown hair. A botanically inspired tattoo rose from a halter top to her right shoulder and down her bicep. Leaning into the front window of a green Chevy Blazer, she was in an animated conversation with the driver. The man behind the wheel gave off a pimp vibe and wore a flat brim cap pulled down over his short hair. His eyes were hidden behind a pair of Oakley sunglasses, and short stubble decorated his acne-scarred chin.

As Cassidy and I got out of the truck, the woman gave a long hard look in our direction. Perhaps eyeing us as potential clientele. I took a quick swig of the rum, handed the bottle to Cassidy, and turned toward the office to check in. A red BMW drove into the lot and parked next to us. The nicest car in the lot by a long shot. A kid in his twenties got out. Brown hair combed conventionally across his head. A boyish face. He wore khaki shorts, a polo shirt, and converse sneakers. Likely a recent college graduate with a big salary and nothing better to spend his money on. As he stood by his car, the woman walked deliberately toward him. She gave a nod of recognition, and he followed her up the stairs to a room on the second floor and disappeared behind a green door with chipping paint.

I made my way to the front office. Inside, everything was tile, stainless steel, or some other easily sterilized surface. It smelled of stale coffee and lemon-scented cleaner. A television set hung lopsidedly from the wall above the desk, spewing content in a torrent of flashing colors and sound bites. A mother with two children was discussing a convoluted issue with the desk clerk. Eventually it was my turn.

"Sorry about that wait," he said. "That lady?" He raised his eyebrows. "She came in here the other day with her two kids." He paused.

"Oh, yeah?" I replied, wondering where he was going with the story. "*Had she stolen a pillow? Smoked in a non-smoking room? Left some illicit drug paraphernalia lying about in the room?*"

"Yeah." He continued his story in a mystified tone. "Well, she got home today and found out her credit card wasn't charged for the room. She was worried we never got the payment. She came in to pay in cash, man." He finished in a crescendo.

"Really, huh?" I said with a grin. "So, there are still honest people in this world."

"Thing is." He began pecking at the keyboard. "We wouldn't have known. I would've just forgot about it."

I signed the litany of standard forms and got our room keys. Outside, Cassidy was digging through the back of his truck. I hadn't been more than 15 minutes inside, but the BMW and its young tech geek were already gone. I forced my brain not to think about what had happened in that room.

The courtesan swaggered in her red heels across the lot to the Chevy Blazer. A gimpy pug bolted from behind the dumpsters and began barking at her. The flat-faced beast sounded like an asthmatic alien in a spawning ritual. At first, she ignored the fiend as he continued his vocal assault from a safe distance. But the insufferable creature doubled down on its insanity, running under her feet as she lit a cigarette.

"Get away from meeeee!" She kicked at the dog, holding the cigarette between her fingers. The unholy terror nipped at her heels. She stopped and bent low. Taking a long drag from the cigarette she stared into the eyes of the pariah dog. "Shut up!" Silvery blue ribbons of smoke rose from her face and lingered in the air above for a fleeting moment. She turned and raced back to the Chevy and, with a final kick of her red heel, jumped into the passenger side.

We watched them peel out of the parking lot as we gathered our bags and went inside. The room smelled slightly of stale cigarette smoke, and a fist-sized hole had been poorly patched in the middle of the bathroom door. We had already missed the meeting's opening social that afternoon, but Cassidy was presenting a poster that evening. We took turns showering and got ready to head downtown. I packed a flask and a water bottle. Cassidy picked up his poster tube, and we set off toward the convention center on foot.

The urban jungle of Portland stood in sharp contrast to my lonely desert sensibilities. Smells from taverns mingled with acrid odors of sewage. Bicyclists and cars jammed up intersections in all directions. Near the convention center, we waited several minutes for a chance to cross the street. Two large glass steeples rose from the otherwise low-profile building.

Inside, smells of fried food wafted in from an unseen kitchen. The floor was covered in floral carpet, and the walls, colored in soft tones, produced an unassuming yet welcoming atmosphere. The poster session was in the grand hall. Rows of poster boards on roller wheels covered the floor and were ready to be stuffed into storage by week's end in preparation for the next event. A campaign rally? A furry convention? A car show? I hadn't the slightest clue.

Toward the back, hundreds of people busily chatted over drinks and hors d'oeuvres. But before we could reach them, we had to traverse a maze of vendors. Sharp dressed and clever, these sales reps stood by their tables, eager to sell us their product, or at least, put us on a mailing list. I had been to small meetings before. I enjoyed the camaraderie among like-minded folks and the shared enthusiasm for obscure science. But this was another beast. In this cacophony of talking heads, we had to squeeze among bodies and poster boards. And if we *did* find a poster of interest, we'd have to interpret the minutia detailed within while an excited author rapped out an overly rehearsed elevator pitch. Answers here would be hard-earned. Solutions to problems, if there were any, would need be divined from this intellectual orgy.

I helped Cassidy find his assigned location, and we pinned his poster to the board. It was nice—he had used stable isotopes to understand how drought affected plants in Sierra Nevada sub-alpine meadows. The brightly colored figures and mountain imagery were sure to attract a crowd. I gave him a nip from my flask before leaving him to the wolves. To prepare for the ensuing madness, I found the nearest drink line. Our registration came with two drink tickets. I could use a beer to supplement the rum.

Already overwhelmed, I wanted to stand someplace quietly for a few minutes and collect my thoughts. Drink in hand, I found an empty table where I could study the program and make mental notes of posters I wanted to check out. The unwieldy abstract list gave me anxiety. Scientists from every corner of the country had descended upon Portland and were all here. I would never get through even a fraction of the information.

"Pot sticker?" chimed a voice next to me.

"Huh…" Startled, I looked up. "Oh, pot sticker. Yes, please." I thanked the server and grabbed three before turning back to my program.

Unfortunately, what appeared to be two faculty members from a nearby college had taken up residence at the table.

"The central *thrust* of my research program is…" one said in a short burst of audible speech. He continued to expound on the core *foci* of his recent investigations. After several failed attempts at interrupting the monologue, the other nodded along in a strained attempt at mild interest.

"*Oh shit,*" I thought. "*I hope he doesn't pull me into his pontifications. What would I have to say?*" I washed down the pot stickers with my beer and made for the posters.

The first aisle I approached was a gauntlet of flailing arms and moving bodies. I took a breath and entered the fracas. Luckily, the chaos was centralized around a few posters. Beyond the fray, a few cagey authors stood alone, nervously awaiting the bedlam that would soon descend upon them. I navigated the confusion and dodged a projectile of seltzer water sent flying by a wildly gesticulating man grilling a student on his statistical methods. I spotted a lone author standing next to her poster; she looked young and anxious but eager. Being that I was sufficiently inebriated at this point and didn't want to startle her, I took a moment to gulp down some water from my bottle before stepping up to her poster: *Bill length in shorebirds across a salt-marsh tidal ecotone.*

"I like your straightforward title," I said. In the confusion of complex problems and elusive answers, I appreciated the elegant simplicity of her study. "So, the birds in the salt marsh have longer bills for catching prey in the mud?" I asked.

"Yes," she said excitedly. "In the salt marsh, birds use relatively longer bills to probe the mud for prey. But in the tidal zone, birds capitalize on prey at or near the surface of the sand—they don't need the longer bill."

Before I could respond, a beer-wielding graduate student burst in on the conversation. Nursing his complimentary drink, he sidled up, furrowed his brow, and scrutinized the poster. I wasn't sure if I should flee or stay and offer support.

He took a sip of his drink and, after a painfully long silence, said, "I see you're using P-values to test null hypotheses."

"Yes, I used a t-test to test for difference in bill length between—" He cut her off mid-sentence.

"Have you considered using a *Bayesian* framework rather than *simple P*-values," he said.

"Ummm, bayes?" She was baffled. "We found a very significant difference in bill length. And a large effect size too," she said.

"Well, I really think this could benefit from a *Bayesian* interpretation." He failed miserably to sound helpful as he looked squarely into her eyes.

"*Jesus*," I thought. I thanked her and escaped as quickly as I could. As much as I wanted to, I didn't have the mental resolve to help this poor student. She had fallen prey to the intellectual analog of the yoked gym jock. Seldom had I witnessed such agonizing human interaction.

My experience in graduate school thus far had been one of initial grandiose ambition quickly replaced by self-doubt. But, for some, the title of "graduate student" produces delusions of grandeur. Usually a guy, he is armed with a sense of superiority after passing *Intro to Advanced Statistical Analysis* with a B+. To further fan his inflated ego, he has misinterpreted his advisor's hands-off approach as a signal that she thinks he is capable of independent scientific thinking. This intellectual narcissist prowls the edge of poster sessions, slowly consuming his allotted free beverage. Like a nascent predator, he looks for an unsuspecting mark. Tragically, this all too often is a single-looking young woman. Perhaps he hopes to seduce her with his cerebral prowess?

This awkward scene was unfolding quickly, and I couldn't get away fast enough. Unfortunately, I discovered my escape path was blocked. A precocious student with a crew cut was holding court a few posters over, challenging anyone within earshot to a wildlife scat quizlet. Luckily, my flask fell from my pocket as I approached, giving me an opportunity to ignore him as I stooped to pick it up.

I extricated myself from the mayhem and glanced back over my shoulder at the undergrad. Thankfully, a friend had joined her with drinks. They chatted cheerily as the Bayesian guy awkwardly lurked nearby. He would likely loiter another 10 minutes before coming to the painful realization that he had missed his prey.

After a few more distracted chats with poster presenters, I'd seen enough for one night. And as the meeting would go on for the whole week, I wanted to pace myself. I found Cassidy; he was fending off questions from a half-dozen spectators but seemed to be enjoying himself. I told him I was going out for a walk, and I'd see him back at our room.

I stepped into the night. The hum of the urban environment was a welcome reprieve from the pandemonium of the conference. A slight breeze lifted litter into the air. Bicyclists continued in critical mass racing up and down the streets. Thinly dressed women shouldering mats exited a warmly lit yoga studio. The smell of lavender wafted in the air as I passed the entrance. I meandered aimlessly through the city streets.

I passed a homeless shelter. The bitter smell of human filth filled the air. People spilled out the front door of the packed building. Weary employees checked in new occupants as junkies writhed in the agony of withdrawal. Those that didn't fit inside sat on the sidewalk. A woman asked for help. I had no paper money or change. With a wallet full of plastic, I was helpless to help. I continued toward Burnside Bridge and the Willamette River.

A crowd congregated outside a strip club. Flashing lights and blasts of house music radiated from within each time a bouncer opened the door. The smell of cigarette smoke drifted in the air. A menagerie of young men eagerly awaited their turn for some kind of satisfaction.

The contemporary Portland I had heard so much about was allegedly a mecca of liberal thinking and self-awareness. An experiment in progressive idealism in a world apparently afraid of change. Like the meeting, this Portland was an epicenter of progressive minds, seeking answers in a world of disorder. But historical Portland is stained with white-supremacy and racism. The Ku Klux Klan had an early influence in local and statewide politics, and those early days of discrimination seemed to me to be reflected in the white-washed population of hipsters on fixed gears worrying about their carbon footprint. Despite farm-to-table cafes and pay-as-you-like yoga studios, human suffering still lurked in the shadows.

I reached Burnside Bridge. Wind blew off the water below and chilled me as I strolled along the sidewalk. Constructed nearly one hundred years ago, the iconic bridge itself is an artifact of Portland's unsavory past. Pushed through by dirty commissioners who were backed by the Klan, the bridge was built on properties they owned, and they raked in small fortunes on the graft. The bridge, now only one of many, connects two sides of the city. A city testing the limits of liberalism. Could this place erase its past? Would any of us find the answers we sought? Or would we only be left with new questions?

A pickup truck blew by. Engine roaring and diesel smoke spewing from its exhaust pipe. A Trump banner flapped from its bed. A stark reminder that Oregon is more than one city. An indication of growing tension. A sign that the minority political bloc, small as it may be, stands in radical opposition to the surrounding liberal haven. A tinder box. Like the desiccated forests of the Northwest, needing only a spark to unleash the furies of Hell upon the land.

A Small Recycling Operation

THE WIND whipped several plastic bags 20 feet into the air before they settled back to the ground, getting caught in cheatgrass and rocks. A sign along the dirt road cautioned: "Slow, Tortoise Zone. 15 mph." To the south, solar panels cut through the plain for half a mile, their metallic faces turned west, tracking the sun. Where they ended, the desert stretched out until broken once more by white wind turbines dotting the foothills of the southern Sierra Nevada. Ahead of me, Cassidy's truck kicked up dust that moved quickly in the northerly wind as we caravanned higher into Pine Tree Canyon. We passed under the white pipe of the smaller of two aqueducts that Los Angeles used to tap the water of the Owens Valley. Nearby two salt cedars rose 40 feet into the air, providing the only meaningful shelter from the sun for miles. Their branches danced in the wind like tendrils. An RV sat parked at the base of the large trees, and a man walked slowly back and forth within the drawn-out shadow cast by the late afternoon sun. A dog looked lazily at us as we rolled by.

Cassidy slowed to a stop, and I drew up beside him. "Let's go up there," I said. I pointed out my window toward the far side of a beige pipeline that rose steeply out of the canyon a quarter mile farther up the road—the larger, original aqueduct for the LA Department of Water and Power. I had researched the area as possible habitat for woodrats and was excited to see what we would find.

"Okay," Cassidy replied out his window. "Oh, hey, have one of these," he said and tossed me a can of Hamm's as he pulled ahead.

"Cheers, buddy," I said as I cracked it open. I moved on at a steady 15 mph. I passed creosote and the occasional Joshua tree as I jammed out to the Grateful Dead on the stereo. Wildflowers had long since bloomed and were now desiccating under the sun. The desert floor glistened with slivers of glass and all manner of debris left behind by target shooters. An empty six-pack of Coors marked the vantage point from which someone had proudly sharpened their lethal craft on a nearby television set.

"Mmmm hmmmm mmm," I hummed along to a Dylan tune as performed by the Dead. Bobby's voice crooned as Jerry dropped back from a solo. "To her, hmmm mm…"

I waited for the next line. And waited. Then, static. And suddenly, "GOD, will bring you from the edge. And, GOD…" a shrill voice let the words hang for a moment before continuing, "will lift you up. And, GOD, will save you from your sin."

"Oh, dammit," I shouted and slapped the dash. I checked the radio while the whiny voice of a middle-aged white Southern man pleaded for Faith Gifts from his listeners.

"Christian radio," I said aloud as I adjusted the tuning on the radio. "Way out here in the middle of nowhere! It's always the Christian stations that come in. Not even country! I'd be okay with some country. Maybe some Waylon Jennings or Merle Haggard. Hell, we're in Kern County," I said.

I gathered myself and continued to a large round clearing in the desert scrub where we parked. Outside, Cassidy began stretching out against the tailgate of his truck. He grimaced as he twisted his back. The blackened rocks of a fire pit stood 40 feet away and within a larger ring of bare Earth and trash. Glass, plastic, partially decayed cardboard boxes that once contained any number of convenience-store items. The detritus had even accumulated into layers, several inches thick, of human filth. I imagined some archaeology grad student in the far away future. *"Poor bastard will be left studying ancient society based on smashed television sets and the desiccated skeletons of lawn furniture,"* I thought. A grungy jackrabbit fled the scene as I closed the truck door.

"Jesus Christ." Cassidy gesticulated as he surveyed the scene. He continued mumbling as he walked into the desert looking for a bush to water. He came back with a stack of orange clay pigeons that had survived the firing squad and placed them on a boulder next to the fire ring. "They can't recycle... They can't clean up after themselves... They can't keep a job... People are slobs..." He trailed off.

"Ya know," I said as I inspected my truck tires. "My dumb *ass* drove right into this Godforsaken trash. That's a real good way to get *four* flat tires."

"Looks like about the best spot to camp for the night, though," Cassidy said as he cracked open a beer.

"Well, my tires are fine. Looks like I got lucky this time." I stood up and pulled gear from the back of my truck. I looked over my shoulder back toward the dry wash. "You see the woodrat nests down yonder?"

"No, where?" Cassidy asked, his voice stifled. He was halfway inside the bed of his truck, legs sticking out the back.

"Down in the wash. They're nesting in the desert almond shrubs," I said.

"Oh, sweet," said Cassidy. He had now extracted himself from his truck and was unfolding a camp chair. He looked toward the wash.

"What do you want for dinner? I can make burritos," I said.

I waited for a response but didn't get one. Then I heard the clackity-clack of a loose muffler.

"Oh, man," Cassidy said. "Why don't I like the look of this guy coming up the road."

An old white Chevy pickup pulled up. Its transmission strained. Inside, a strung-out tweaker with facial tattoos sat in the driver's seat. A woman next to him. The cab's rear window was smashed out, and an emaciated gold and white pit bull peered at us from the truck bed.

"Hey there, fellas," he said thickly. A hand-rolled cigarette bounced up and down as he mouthed the words. Thin wisps of smoke rose up and out the truck window. "Sorry to roll up on ya like this," he continued, the cigarette glued to his lip.

I gave Cassidy a discreet glance. He stood squarely facing the truck but said nothing. I didn't know what this guy wanted and wasn't sure I wanted to hang around long enough to find out.

"Ya'll seen any brass out here?" the man asked unintelligibly. He pulled another cigarette from behind his ear and lit it on the ember of the first.

"*Grass?*" I thought. "*Did he ask if we'd seen grass? Pretty sure no one's tryin' to grow weed out here.*"

"Sorry, not sure I can help you," I said.

Cassidy glanced out over the thousands of shell-casings littering the ground and scratched his head—looking somewhat relieved. "You said brass?" he asked.

"See, my ass is in a sling here," the man explained as he opened the truck door and slowly slid from the driver's seat. "I gotta be up in Lone Pine tomorrow, and I ain't got no money," arms waving as he said the words.

"Sorry," Cassidy said warily.

"Well." The man paused as he surveyed the area through squinted eyes. "A buddy of mine works for LADWP says there's enough brass out here to fill a five-gallon bucket." The woman eased herself out of the passenger side of the truck.

"Well, have at it," I said. "There's a shitload of shells here. Also, up and over that hill," I pointed to the west. "Plenty of target shooters go up there too."

He lifted a bucket from the truck bed, and the woman, bent over and pacing slowly, stared at the ground. The pit bull hopped out to inspect my box of food.

A sense of relief coursed through my veins. I still wasn't certain we wouldn't be mugged, or worse. But the pair seemed much less nefarious now as they scavenged through the residue of consumerism. The man continued to mumble, and I wasn't sure if he was talking to us anymore.

"I owe this guy a hundred bucks, ya see," he said as he carried off the bucket. "... Gene Autry Lane up there." I couldn't quite hear what he was saying. "... Just need a little gas money...used car lot..." His voice faded as he walked away.

Cassidy glanced over at me and grinned. "Wanna grab a couple beers and walk up the canyon a bit?"

"I'm already one step ahead," I said as I pulled two from the cooler. "Just lock up." I smiled as I handed him a Hamm's.

Shopping bags stuck on creosote bushes waved like derelict flags in the wind. The day's final rounds of gunfire echoed off the canyon walls in the distance. Bullet shells and fragments of bottles glinted in the setting sun. Above, buzzing nighthawks picked off flying insects in midair.

We reached the top of a small crag. Inside its cracks, woodrats had stuffed sticks, rocks, and trash collected from the desert floor below. We sat against the warm stone. The eastern sky faded from pastel orange to purple. In the valley far below the canyon, solar arrays reflecting sunlight looked like small geometric bodies of water. A surreal image in the arid Mojave Desert. Half a mile downcanyon, the aqueduct glowed red as it rose to the canyon rim, its precious contents sheltered from the dry desert air, destined for LA. I took a long drink from the cold beer and tucked the can in a small nook in the stone, taking care the wind would not blow it over. Below, the couple worked the desert floor. The clatter of brass in the metal pail punctuated the silence. Hunched over and moving in haphazard semi-circles, they sifted through litter and debris. Cobbling together a minute fortune, piece by piece, from the discarded waste of the careless.

Acknowledgments

I have many people to thank for the creation and inspiration of this book. I would not have written these stories without the encouragement of so many friends and strangers. Steve Lee, Michael Cleaver, and Steve Anderson have provided many hours of open ears as they listened to my ramblings and encouraged my writing journey. Anne Espeset and Josh Jahner provided valuable feedback on early drafts of some of these stories. In all the nooks and crannies of the American West, it has been my great pleasure to meet, make friends with, and simply observe the denizens of the desert that forge a living in these beautiful yet rugged landscapes.

I thank my family who have influenced my way of viewing the world and have profoundly impacted my life for the better. My mom, Marty, nurtured my sense of creativity and wonder in the world. My dad, Brent, also a scientist, stimulated my analytical side. I also thank my three brothers: Peter, Ben, and Greg, whom I am privileged to call best friends. We don't all live close together, and frequent visits are challenging in adult life, but the bonds we built in childhood have kept us connected, and our mutual love has enriched my life.

I also thank my major advisors: Dr. Heather Bateman and Dr. Marjorie Matocq. The travels and experiences I enjoyed during my graduate school years form the bedrock of this entire book. Through their support and dedication to science and understanding the natural world, I was given the opportunity to become intimately acquainted with corners of the American West that are often overlooked and underappreciated.

I also thank Mary Whitfield, director of the Southern Sierra Research Station, for her hospitality during my time at nearby field locations. Her enthusiasm for the birds and other wildlife of the region was always an inspiration. And I thank Reed Tollefson, manager of the Kern River Preserve, for always clearing us a place to camp and for introducing me to other important members of the local community.

To my editor, Jennifer Crittenden, for the boundless patience, encouragement, and excitement she has given this project. Thank you. When I first imagined this collection of stories, it was a shapeless idea in my mind. You gave this shape, and a life.

And finally, I thank Sunny and Skylar. For your love, and for putting up with me. My world is immeasurably richer with you in it.

About the Author

Danny Nielsen spent his childhood exploring the woods of Alabama before moving to Utah in high school. Culture shock quickly wore off as he developed a love, perhaps an addiction, for sweeping desert vistas and mountain skylines. He has spent the last decade traveling the American West for research and pleasure, studying and writing about its flora and fauna, including the human characters that make their home there. Danny lives in Reno and is a PhD student at the University of Nevada, Reno. *Straight Flossin' and Other Stories of the American West* is his first book.

About the Illustrator

Sunny Noel Sawyer studied Ecology and Evolution at University of California, Davis, where she minored in Art Studio. As a native Californian, she is inspired by the beauty and complexity of western landscapes. She is a physician assistant in Reno, Nevada and produces art in a variety of mediums in her spare time.